Revolution in France

**The era of the French Revolution
and Napoleon, 1789–1815**

Josh Brooman

Longman Group UK Limited Longman House,
Burnt Mill, Harlow, Essex, CM20 2JE, England
and Associated Companies throughout the World.

First published 1992
Fourth impression 1993
ISBN 0 582 08254 4

Set in 11/15pt Bodoni (Lasercomp)
Printed in Hong Kong
SC/04

Designed by: Roger Walton Studio
Illustrated by: John Laing, Sue Sharples
Cover photograph: *Attack on the Bastille* (detail)
painted by Charles Thevenin, 1795. Musée
Carnavalet, Paris (photo: Bulloz).

We are indebted to Oxford University Press for
permission to reproduce an English lullaby from
Oxford Dictionary of Nursery Rhymes by Iona
and Peter Opie (pub 1951).

**The Publisher's policy is to use paper
manufactured from sustainable forests.**

We are grateful to the following for permission to
reproduce photographs:

By gracious permission of Her Majesty Queen
Elizabeth II, page 19

Associated Press (Photo: J. Widener), page 91;
front page of *Avanti*: 1 May 1901, page 90 *left*;
The Barber Institute of Fine Arts, University of
Birmingham, page 5 *above right*; Biblioteca
Estense, Modena (Bridgeman Art Library), page
16; Bridgeman Art Library, pages 41, 78,
(Giraudon), page 17; British Museum, London,
pages 31, 34, 42; Charlottenburg Castle, Berlin
(Bridgeman Art Library Fabri), page 60; Château
de Versailles (Bridgeman Art Library/Giraudon),
pages 5 *below right*, 15, 24, 53, 56, 58–9, 68–9, 74,
92 (Bulloz) pages 22, 77, (Réunion des Musées
Nationaux), page 40; Christie's, London
(Bridgeman Art Library), page 5 *above left*; taken
from Denis Diderot & Jean le Rond d'Alembert,
L'Encyclopédie: Receuil de planches . . . .
1762–72, page 6; © Documentation Française
(Photo: Holzapfel), page 87; Edimedia, page 14;
Metropolitan Museum of Art, New York,
Purchase, Mr & Mrs Charles Wrightsman Gift,

1977, page 13; Musée Carnavalet, Paris
(Bridgeman Art Library/Giraudon), pages 8
above, 25, 30, 45, 49, 83, (Bulloz) pages 29, 88,
(E.T. Archive) page 33, (Photothèque des Musées
de la Ville de Paris, © DACS 1992) pages 8
below, 18, 36, 38, 39 , 43, 48; Musée Dauphinois,
Grenoble, page 20; Musée de l'Art Wallon, Liège,
page 86; Musée de la Révolution Française,
Vizille, pages 50, 51; Musée de la Ville de
Strasbourg, page 72; Musée des Arts Décoratifs,
Paris, page 5 *below left*; Musée des Beaux-Arts,
Lyon, page 63; Musée des Beaux-Arts, Nantes
(Bridgeman Art Library/Giraudon) page 46;
Musée d'Orsay, Paris (Bridgeman Art
Library/Giraudon) page 79; Musée du Louvre,
Paris (Bridgeman Art Library/Giraudon) pages
64–5, 89; Musée du Petit Palais, Paris
(Bridgeman Art Library/Giraudon) page 94; The
National Museums and Galleries on Merseyside
(Walker Art Gallery, Liverpool) page 61;
Picturepoint, page 90 *right*; Roger-Viollet, page
12; Spectrum Colour Library, pages 84, 93; Tate
Gallery, London (John Webb) page 80.

Contents

1 France before the Revolution

Throughout the summer of 1789 millions of normally law-abiding French people took part in a violent revolution. In cities, towns and villages all over France, men and women used violence to change the way they lived. By the end of the year they had destroyed their centuries-old system of law and government. In the decade that followed, they would go on to transform their society, their religion and their economy.

What made ordinary men and women behave like this? Why did they want to destroy the old system of government and society? This chapter tries to answer those questions by showing how their country was organised and run in the years shortly before 1789.

French people and their society

The pictures opposite show just a few of the 28 million people who lived in France shortly before the Revolution.

In one way the pictures are similar. Each shows a family at home. But a quick look at the details shows that these families lived very different lives. It soon becomes clear that each belonged to a different social class.

1 Choose one of the pictures opposite. What does it tell you about the lives of the people it portrays?

2 How can you tell from pictures 1–4 that each family belonged to a different social class?

1 A family of peasants painted by Jean-François Clermont. About 20 million French people were peasants – country people who made their living by farming.

2 A family of town workers painted in 1775 by Etienne Aubry. About 2 million people worked in towns – for example, shopkeepers, traders, craftsmen, builders and labourers.

3 A *bourgeois* family painted in 1787 by Louis Léopold Boilly. Some 2 million people belonged to the *bourgeoisie* – the well-to-do 'middle class' between the nobility and the workers and peasants. This family, the Gohins of Rouen, were ship-owners.

4 A noble family painted by Louis Michel van Loo (1707–71). The Duke of Penthièvre and his family are drinking chocolate. The nobility was the land-owning, ruling class. They had titles such as Duke, Marquis, or Viscount to distinguish them from 'commoners' – that is, everyone else in society. Between 120,000 and 350,000 people were nobles.

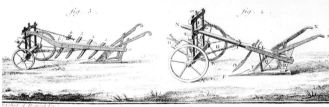

Agriculture, Labourage.

5 Illustrations from the *Encyclopédie*, published in France in the 1760s, show a wide variety of French people at work.

The three estates

The short exercise on pages 4 and 5 will have shown you that most French people belonged to four social classes: the peasantry, the town working class, the middle class or *bourgeoisie*, and the nobility.

In practice, however, society wasn't so simple. According to French law, people did not belong to classes but to **estates**. The law said there were three estates. In the first were the clergy – people who made a living by working in the Church. In the second were the nobility. And in the third was everybody else.

This mattered because people in the first and second estates (the clergy and nobility) had privileges, or rights, which gave them a number of advantages. Of greatest value were their financial privileges which let them off paying certain taxes. Source 6 shows who did and did not have privileges:

1 **What kind of work are the people doing in each picture in source 5?**
2 **Judging by source 6, what did these people have in common?**
3 **Judging by the pictures, what did they *not* have in common?**

6	First estate About 130,000 people	The clergy: • 138 archbishops and bishops • 2,800 canons and priors • 37,000 nuns and 23,000 monks • 60,000 parish priests	Main privileges: • had their own law courts • did not have to pay certain taxes
	Second estate Between 120,000 and 350,000 people	The nobility: • the king and queen • nobles of the sword: princes of royal blood, dukes, marquises, counts, viscounts, barons, knights • nobles of the robe	Main privileges: • had the right to carry a sword • got special treatment in law courts • did not have to pay certain taxes • did not have to do military service
	Third estate About 27 million people	Everybody else: e.g. lawyers, doctors, businessmen, merchants, soldiers, craftsmen, shopkeepers, peasants	Privileges: None

The three estates had once been important in French society. Back in the middle ages, nobles had been soldiers with the job of fighting for France in wartime. The clergy ran the country's education and religious life. In return for this important work, the king had given the nobles and clergy their own estates and privileges.

By 1789, however, the nobles and clergy were less important than they had been in the middle ages. Nobles, for example, no longer had the sole

7 *Let's hope this game will soon be over*: two popular engravings of 1789.

Choose one of the cartoons in source 7:
1 Identify the estate to which each person belonged.
2 Using the information about the three estates in source 6, say what point you think the artist was trying to make.

responsibility for war. Most French people therefore thought the system of estates was outdated and unfair. Their view can be seen in source 7.

Poverty

You have seen that the division of people into three estates was unequal in numbers and in privileges. But this wasn't the only inequality in French society. Many other divisions kept people apart.

By far the greatest inequality in French society was in people's wealth. While some of the nobles and the *bourgeoisie* were incredibly rich, most people were poor. In a book about Paris, an eighteenth-century French writer described the conditions in which many working people lived:

8 An entire family lives in a single room, in which the four walls are bare, the beds have no covers, and the kitchen things are piled up with the chamber pots. All the furniture together is not worth twenty crowns*. Every three months the inhabitants are thrown out for owing back rent and must find another hole to live in. Thus, they wander, taking their miserable possessions from refuge to refuge.

Louis-Sebastien Mercier, *Tableau de Paris* [Picture of Paris], 1783
* roughly £120 in present-day prices

Several million people were so poor that they had to rely on charity to stay alive. Some of them are described in the records of a charity office in a town in southern France:

9 Pierre N, shoemaker, aged 70, almost blind, his wife the same age . . . Jacques Notre, day labourer, widower, aged 30, ill for a week with a continuous fever, two children who are under six, and very poor . . . Jean N, day labourer aged 45; his wife of the same age, having five children, the eldest in service, a girl of twelve who is blind, another of ten, the others two and four . . . Yves N, aged 12, blind and paralysed in one leg, cannot walk, carried to the parish from four miles away to beg . . . Françoise N, orphan, age 12, employed at putting cows to graze, had neither linen nor clothes, almost naked, and has no means to cover herself because those who employ her out of charity are almost as poor as she is.

Règlemens Des Bureaux de Charité, Aix-en-Provence [Regulations of the Charity Offices of Aix-en-Provence], date unknown

In 1790 a government committee worked out that a family of five needed at least 435 *livres* (pounds) a year to provide for its basic needs. Other than food, it listed these as:

3 Judging by source 9, what kinds of people were the poorest members of French society?
4 Study sources 10 and 11. What do they tell you about a) the home lives, and b) the food of people on very low incomes in 1789?

10

Rent of a fourth- or fifth-floor room	45 *livres**
Clothing	80 *livres*
Heating	36 *livres*
Purchase and upkeep of chattels [belongings]	24 *livres*
Utensils, soap, candles or lamp oil	15 *livres*
Capitation tax	2 *livres*
Total	202 *livres*

From the 5th report of the Charity Committee, 1 Sept. 1790

That left 233 livres a year to buy food – around 13 *sous** a day. This list of prices in Paris shops for June 1790 shows what you could buy with that:

11

	livres	sous		livres	sous
Bread (4-pound loaf)	—	11	Eggs (per 10)	—	8½
Wine (per litre)	—	10	Rice (per pound)	—	8½
Beef (per pound)	—	11	Olive oil (per pound)	—	9
Veal (per pound)	—	11½	Sugar (per pound)	1	4
Mutton (per pound)	—	14	Coffee (per pound)	1	14
Butter (per pound)	—	14	Candles (per pound)	—	15
Firewood (56 cubic feet)	21	12			

Adapted from George Rudé, *Prices, Wages and Popular Movements in Paris during the French Revolution*, 1954

*In present-day prices, one *livre* is equivalent to about £2 and one *sou* to about 10 pence.

Unequal taxation

Although most people were poor, they still had to pay taxes. Then, as now, there were two kinds of tax – taxes paid directly to the government, and indirect taxes which people paid whenever they bought certain goods.

The average family paid between 10% and 15% of its yearly earnings in tax to the government. Some, however, were exempt from some taxes. In other words, they did not have to pay them. You can see from the table on the following page who did and who did not have to pay the main taxes:

12 **Principal taxes in France in the 1780s**

	Name	Type of tax	Who was meant to pay	Who was exempt
Direct taxes	*Taille*	A tax on either land or income	All citizens (except men on army service)	Nobles, clergy
	Capitation	A poll tax – a fixed sum paid each year to the government	All citizens	Nobody – but, in practice, many nobles and clergy evaded it or paid little
	Twentieths	An income tax of one twentieth of a year's earnings	All citizens	Nobody – but, in practice, nobles and clergy evaded it or paid little
	Corvée	A labour tax requiring unpaid work mending royal roads	All able-bodied men	Nobles, clergy, townspeople, post masters, country school-teachers, shepherds
Indirect taxes	*Gabelle*	A tax on salt	Anybody buying salt	3.3 million people living in four exempt provinces
	Octroi	A tax, paid at the town gates, on goods being taken to market	The merchant who transported the goods	Nobody was exempt
	Aides	A tax on drinks, especially wine	Anybody buying wine etc.	Some provinces were exempt
	Traites	A tax on goods being transported from one province to another	The merchant who transported the goods	Nobody was exempt

1 **Find out what direct and indirect taxes people in this country today have to pay.**
2 **What similarities and differences are there between present-day taxes and eighteenth-century French taxes?**

You can see from the table above that nobles and clergy were exempt from many taxes. Even when they did pay taxes, they paid no more than anyone else. Rich people therefore had no difficulty in paying tax.

In addition to paying taxes to the government, millions of peasants also had to pay money to their landlords. Most nobles and many of the clergy were landlords, or *seigneurs*. They owned land which they rented to peasants to farm. As tenants, the peasants owed dues to their landlords. The table on the next page shows just a few of those **feudal rights and dues**.

The most common feudal rights and dues

13

Rights	The right of the oven	Peasants had to bake their bread in an oven owned by the landlord, paying a fee for its use.
	The right of the mill	Peasants had to grind their corn in the landlord's windmill or watermill, paying a fee to use it.
	The right of the press	Peasants had to press their grapes in the landlord's grape-press, paying a fee for its use.
	The right of the hunt	The landlord could ride over his tenants' fields while hunting, even if they were planted.
	The right of the warren	The landlord could keep rabbits in a warren. Tenants could not kill them even when they damaged their crops.
	The right of the dovecote	The landlord could keep pigeons in a dovecote. Tenants could not kill them even when they damaged their crops.
	Market rights	Peasants had to pay a tax on produce which they took to markets held on the lord's land.
Dues	The *corvée*	Peasants had to do several days' unpaid work for the landlord each year – for example, helping to bring in the landlord's harvest.
	The *cens*	Peasants had to pay a tax to the landlord each year.
	The *champart*	Peasants had to give the landlord a portion of their crops each year.

As well as paying feudal dues, everyone in a parish had to give the Church a **tithe**. This meant giving the local church around a tenth of their yearly income or produce.

Paying dues and tithes was easier for some people than for others. A well-to-do tenant farmer could usually make enough money at market to pay without difficulty. A poor farm labourer, however, could only pay in kind – that is, by handing over part of his hard-earned crop. The picture on page 12 shows this.

12

14 *It can't go on for ever!* A French cartoon of 1789.

To which social class does the man with a pack belong?

2 In his pack are a spade, some vegetables and a flail (used for threshing crops). In his hands are a lantern and a hoe. Suggest what the artist wanted us to think about him.

3 Who are the other two men? What connection might they have with the third man?

4 What, in your view, is the message of this picture?

Critics of French society

Most French people did not question the way their society was organised. It may have been unequal and unfair, but most knew no other way of life.

A handful of educated people, however, did question it. They were the *philosophes*, a group of writers, journalists and scientists who shared a way of thinking which they called Reason. They believed that the only way to know if something was true was to observe and test it. They refused to accept anything as true without questioning it.

A *philosophe* at work

A good example of a *philosophe* was the scientist Lavoisier, shown in the painting opposite. Lavoisier became famous by discovering how things burn. Most scientists at that time believed that anything which burned contained a substance called phlogiston. Wood, they thought, was a mixture of phlogiston and wood ash. When it burned, the phlogiston vanished, leaving the ash behind.

During the 1770s and 1780s, Lavoisier studied the process of burning to find out whether the theory was correct. After many experiments he decided it was wrong. He suggested instead that things burned when burning material combined with a recently-discovered gas. He named this gas oxygen.

In addition to his scientific work, Lavoisier involved himself in social and political issues. For example, he built an experimental farm on his estate to try

15 Antoine-Laurent de Lavoisier (1743–94), and his wife Anne-Marie, painted in 1788 by Jacques-Louis David.

out new farming methods, hoping to show farmers how to improve their crops. In 1787 he proposed a number of reforms to help the poor. These included abolishing the *taille*, introducing old age pensions and building new hospitals.

The Calas affair

The most famous of the *philosophes* was the writer Voltaire. He especially questioned the power and beliefs of the French Church. He showed his views most clearly when he became involved in a sad case of injustice – the Calas affair.

Jean Calas, a cloth merchant, was a Protestant, living among Catholics in the city of Toulouse. In 1761 one of his sons hanged himself in his father's

16 A seventeenth-century print showing a man being broken on a cartwheel. Continued use of this method of execution in the eighteenth century horrified Voltaire and many other thinking people.

L'oeil toujours surveillant de la divine Arée, *Lors que tenant l'espée et la Balance en main,* *Qui guette les passans les meurtrit et s'en jouë,*
Bannit entierement le dueil d'vne contrée. *Elle juge et punit le voleur inhumain;* *Puis luy mesme devient le jouet d'vne rouë.*

Paris Chez Jean Baptiste Bonnart rue S.t Jacques au Coq.

warehouse. When the body was found, local Catholics gathered outside. A rumour spread that Jean Calas had murdered the boy to stop him converting to the Catholic faith. This seemed believable because another of his sons had already become a Catholic. The magistrates accepted the rumour as true and condemned Jean Calas to death. In public, Calas was tied to a cartwheel and his limbs smashed with an iron bar. He was then strangled and his body burned.

Voltaire believed that Jean Calas was innocent. He said that the magistrates found him guilty simply because he was a Protestant. Over the next three years he carried out a campaign to clear the name of Calas. As a result of his campaign, an appeal court in 1765 found Calas not guilty and pardoned him.

Voltaire took up the Calas case because he thought it showed up some major wrongs in French society. One was religious intolerance – the refusal to allow non-Catholics to follow their own religion. The other was the cruelty of the law which allowed Calas to be tortured to death.

Changes in public opinion

As a result of the writings of *philosophes* such as Voltaire, public opinion began to change. By the 1780s most educated people agreed on a number of basic ideas and values. They wanted a more humane, torture-free system of law. They favoured toleration of non-Catholics such as Protestants and Jews. Above all, they wanted changes in the way France was governed. They wanted a say in how the country was run.

17 The Palace of Versailles painted in 1722 by Jean-Baptiste Martin.

18 Louis XVI, painted in 1775.

19 Marie Antoinette, painted in 1788.

The government of France

France was governed by King Louis the Sixteenth (written as Louis XVI). Louis was an absolute monarch. This meant that he did not have to share his power with anyone else. Unlike King George III of Britain, who shared power with Parliament, Louis could do whatever he chose whenever he pleased.

Louis governed France from the magnificent, thousand-room palace of Versailles, 18km outside Paris. Thousands of nobles lived with him in the palace, serving him as courtiers and helping to run the affairs of the nation.

Louis' wife was Marie Antoinette, an Austrian archduchess. They had married in 1770 when she was fourteen and he was fifteen. At first they had been popular with the French public. As the years went by, however, they lost popularity. People especially disliked Marie Antoinette.

Marie Antoinette

People disliked Marie Antoinette for many reasons. One was the fact that she was foreign. They called her the 'Austrian woman' which, in French, could be made to sound like 'bitch' (*Autrichienne* = Austrian, *chienne* = bitch). People also disliked her for spending huge amounts of money on clothes, jewellery and gambling, for having favourites at court, and, especially, because they thought she was unfaithful to Louis.

Did Marie Antoinette deserve her bad reputation? Let us look at one of

What do pictures 17, 18 and 19 tell you about the French monarchy in the eighteenth century?

20 Marie Antoinette's village in the garden of the Petit Trianon at Versailles.

the reasons for it. In 1774 Louis gave Marie Antoinette her own small palace in the grounds of the palace of Versailles. It was called the Petit Trianon. Over the next five years, Antoinette spent huge sums of money creating beautiful gardens around the Petit Trianon. In part of the garden she built a village, known as the hamlet, of eight thatched cottages, with a barn, stables, and dairy. All were made to look old and run-down, like a real village. In the fields were sheep, goats and cows.

Many people at the time thought the whole idea of the farm was pointless and silly. Even one of her most loyal courtiers thought so. He wrote:

21 A lot of money has been put into making the queen's hamlet look like a poor village. Perhaps by spending a bit more, her majesty would have been able to get rid of the signs of poverty in the real villages for twenty or thirty miles around, and to improve honest people's homes . . . To imitate, in an amusement garden, the suffering of your subjects seems to be making a game out of their situation.

The Marquis de Bombelles, *Journal*, 1780–84

People ever since, like this historian, have agreed with that criticism:

22 It was thought advisable to imitate the poverty and decay of the actual homes of the peasants. Cracks were made in the walls; the plaster was romantically chipped away in patches . . . Hubert Robert, the famous painter, painted cracks in the woodwork to make it look old; and the chimneys were carefully smoked. But, inside, these seemingly tumbledown cottages were equipped with every possible convenience, with mirrors and stoves, with billiard tables and with comfortable couches . . . This hamlet, today a lovely ruin, was for Marie Antoinette a

23 Marie Antoinette, dressed as a shepherdess, looks after new-born lambs.

charming out-of-doors theatre . . . At a time when, throughout France, the unhappy peasants were beginning to grow riotous . . . sheep were led to pasture by ribbons of blue silk tied around their necks.

Stefan Zweig, *Marie Antoinette*, 1933

Not everyone criticised Marie Antoinette for building the village. For example, her foster-brother wrote in his memoirs that:

24 Twelve rustic habitations [cottages] were built at Trianon on the queen's orders. [In these] she settled twelve poor families, taking upon herself to provide them with constant maintenance.

Joseph Weber, *Memoirs of Maria Antoinetta*, 1805

Some modern historians have also defended Marie Antoinette:

25 It is wholly mistaken to see the hamlet as a toy. On the contrary, like her aunt's farm, it belongs in the context of new attempts to improve agriculture . . . The farm was run on commercial lines and brought in on average 6,000 *livres* per year.

Vincent Cronin, *Louis and Antoinette*, 1974

1 Judging by sources 21–23, why did Marie Antoinette's hamlet help to give her a bad reputation?

2 Judging by sources 20–25, did she deserve this reputation?

26 **A sealed letter signed by Louis XV in 1765, ordering the imprisonment of a man named Jugones in the Bastille, a prison in Paris.**

Use and abuse of power

It wasn't only Marie Antoinette who made the royal government unpopular. Many people disliked it because they thought the king had too much power.

An example of what they disliked was the king's use of 'sealed letters' (*lettres de cachet*). A sealed letter was a royal warrant ordering the imprisonment or exile of the person named on it. It was written on a single sheet of paper, signed by the king, folded, and sealed with wax. The person whose name appeared on it stayed in prison or in exile for as long as the king wished.

People hated sealed letters more than any other aspect of the king's power. They especially hated the fact that the king's ministers could use them. As one minister wrote to another in 1752:

27 I am instructed by His Majesty to send you these six letters that you can use as you see fit. You only have to write in the names of those to be arrested.

Letter from the Comte de Saint-Florentin, Secretary of State, to the Duc de Chaulnes, King's Commissioner in Brittany, 1752

People everywhere complained bitterly about sealed letters. In a written protest to the king, Paris lawyers complained that:

28 These orders signed by Your Majesty are often full of names that Your Majesty can never have known. They are there because your ministers have put them there. None of your subjects is safe from the vengeance of a minister.

Remonstrance of the Court of Aids, Paris, 1770

And people in a little town called Bar complained that:

29 Sealed letters are a frightening and cruel attack on the liberty of citizens and on public safety. We demand an end to their use.

List of grievances of the Third Estate of Bar-sur-Seine, 1789

During the reign of Louis XVI, around 14,000 sealed letters were issued, mainly against people who disagreed with the government. Some were sent into exile in distant parts of France. Others were put into royal prisons such as the Bastille in Paris.

Sealed letters were only one of the ways in which the King could impose his authority. A great range of other powers allowed him to do what he liked whenever and wherever he liked. As time went by, more and more people criticised this, and accused Louis of being a 'despot'. This was the eighteenth-century way of saying that a ruler was a dictator, or tyrant.

Judging by sources 27 and 28, suggest why the people of Bar thought that sealed letters were 'frightening and cruel'.

Financial problems

The royal debt

As king of one of the world's largest countries, Louis had to deal with many serious problems. The most urgent problem facing him was the fact that his government was deeply in debt.

The French government had been in debt for nearly a hundred years. This was because it spent more each year than it received in taxes. The diagram below shows just how serious the debt problem was by 1786.

In 1786 the government minister in charge of finances, Calonne, informed Louis that the government was close to financial collapse. Something had to be done quickly to avoid bankruptcy. They must either increase taxes, or reduce their spending, or borrow more money.

30 Charles Alexandre de Calonne, Minister of Finance from 1783 to 1787, painted by Elisabeth Vigée Lebrun.

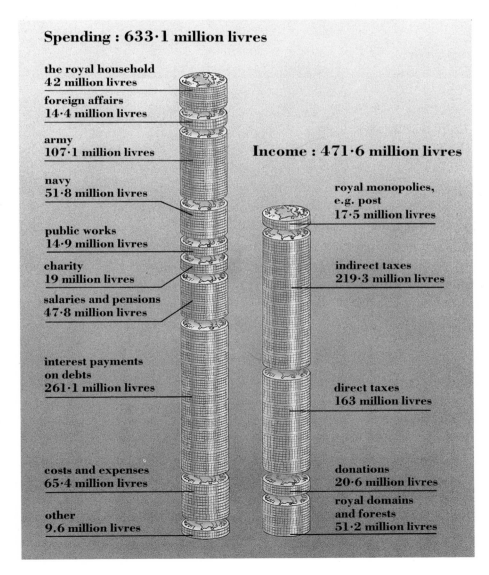

Spending : 633·1 million livres

the royal household
42 million livres

foreign affairs
14·4 million livres

army
107·1 million livres

navy
51·8 million livres

public works
14·9 million livres

charity
19 million livres

salaries and pensions
47·8 million livres

interest payments
on debts
261·1 million livres

costs and expenses
65·4 million livres

other
9·6 million livres

Income : 471·6 million livres

royal monopolies,
e.g. post
17·5 million livres

indirect taxes
219·3 million livres

direct taxes
163 million livres

donations
20·6 million livres

royal domains
and forests
51·2 million livres

31 The French finances in 1788.

How much was the government's debt in 1786? (Take away its income from its spending.)
What did the government spend most money on?
Which of these do you think was the best way of reducing the debt:
a) increasing taxes, b) reducing the government's spending, or c) borrowing more money?

32 The Day of Tiles in Grenoble, 7 June 1788, painted by Alexandre Debelle. The painting shows townspeople protesting against Louis XVI's decision to exile the *Parlements* of Paris, Grenoble and other cities.

An attempt at reform

The exercise on page 19 should have shown you that the government had only one way of avoiding bankruptcy. It would have to raise taxes. Calonne, the finance minister, drew up a plan to reform the tax system. The biggest change would be a tax on land which all landowners would have to pay.

Introducing this land tax would not be easy, however. The nobles and clergy, who were exempt from most taxes, would do all they could to get out of paying it. They could refuse to register it in the Paris law courts, or *Parlement*, which they controlled. As all new laws had to be registered by the Paris *Parlement*, this would delay the new tax from coming into effect.

Hoping to avoid such a delay, Calonne invited 150 leading nobles and clergymen to Paris to discuss and approve the new tax. As only loyal supporters of the king were invited, Calonne thought they would give it their approval without much argument. This 'Assembly of Notables', however, refused to agree to the new tax. They claimed they did not have the power to approve new taxes. They said that only the Estates General, a sort of national parliament elected by all three estates, had that power.

Louis then dismissed the Assembly of Notables and tried to introduce the new tax without their approval. The nobles in the Paris *Parlement*, however, refused to register it. They too said that the only body with the power to agree to new taxes was the Estates General. Louis insisted that he alone had this power, and exiled the entire *Parlement* from Paris.

People everywhere in France protested angrily against this. Some of their protests were violent. In Grenoble, four people died in a 'Day of Tiles' when a mob of protesters pelted soldiers with tiles torn from the city's rooftops.

The protests went on for the next six months. In August 1788, Louis gave in. He ordered elections to be held for an Estates General. The date of its first meeting was to be 1 May 1789.

The Estates General

The nobles and clergy welcomed the king's decision to call an Estates General. They intended to use it to block his plans to tax them. They thought they could do so because of the voting system used by the Estates General.

The voting system

The Estates General met whenever the king wanted to consult it. This was not often. The last time it had met was in 1614. Then, it had been made up of around 750 members, about 250 from each of the three estates. They had met in three separate rooms and, when they voted, each estate had just one vote.

The third estate now complained that this voting system was unfair. If used again in 1789, the nobles and clergy would be able to out-vote the third estate two to one. They asked the king to double their numbers in the Estates General and to give each member one vote each.

In December 1788 the king reluctantly agreed to the first of these demands. By now his government was bankrupt. It could not pay all the interest it owed on its debts. A new finance minister, Jacques Necker, advised him to double the third estate. He hoped that the Estates General itself would decide to give every member one vote each, and then vote for new taxes.

The food crisis

Finance wasn't the only problem facing the government. In the countryside a different kind of crisis was developing: mass hunger.

The crisis was caused by freak weather. On 13 July 1788 a massive hailstorm had destroyed cornfields, vegetable plots, orchards and vineyards all over central France. This was followed by a drought. As a result, the harvest in 1788 was very poor.

This might not have mattered if the weather had gone back to its usual pattern. It did not. The drought was followed by the coldest winter in living memory. Rivers froze over, stopping watermills from grinding flour. Blocked roads prevented food from reaching markets. And when the snow suddenly thawed in the spring, floods ruined huge areas of farmland.

33 Louis XVI giving money to hungry peasants during the winter of 1787–88, painted by Louis Hersent in 1817.

1 Louis is shown in this picture helping his people, yet he was very unpopular in 1788. How can this be explained?

The result of the awful weather was a sharp rise in the price of bread. The price of a loaf rose to 15 *sous* in February 1789. A quick glance at the table on page 9 will show you that poor families were now spending nearly all their earnings just on bread.

With many families spending all they had on bread, they stopped buying things like clothes, shoes, candles and fuel. The factories that made these things lost business, and many workers lost their jobs. Unemployment, added to hunger, led to riots and strikes in many parts of the country.

The complaints lists

With hunger and unemployment spreading, elections for the Estates General were held in spring 1789. As well as electing deputies to speak for them, voters were asked to draw up lists of changes that they wanted the Estates General to discuss with the king.

Over 60,000 of these 'lists of complaints' were drawn up. They showed that millions of French people wanted major changes. Source 34, the complaints list of a village in northern France, is typical of their demands:

Look at source 34.
2 Explain in your own words what the people were complaining about in points 2, 4, 5, 7, 8, 13, and 14.
3 What kind of people do you think made these complaints? Explain your answer.
4 In general, what do the villagers seem to have disliked most about their situation?

34 Complaints list of St Germain sous Cailly
District of Rouen. Population: 57 families.
Seigneur: Madame de Joyeuse

1 We want an end to all taxes and tolls at town gates and their replacement by a single tax.
2 We want tax-free salt.
3 The suppression of begging. Each parish should pay for the relief of poor people's suffering.
4 We want the suppression of the right of the mill.
5 An end to the exemption that nobles enjoy from the *taille* and capitation.
7 We want an adjustment of the tithe.
8 We want a new way of maintaining the main roads. It is most unfair that poor people and others who do not have carriages have to contribute to the upkeep of roads that they never use. It would be fairer if the clergy and nobles were to pay for it.
9 We want the abolition of compulsory service in the army. It deprives workers, old people and the ill of young men on whom they often depend.
10 The right to kill crows . . .
13 The destruction of the rabbit warrens.
14 We want the pigeons to be kept in the dovecote from the start of July until the first of November.
15 We want controls on the price of bread . . .

List of complaints of the Third Estate of the Bailliwick of Rouen for the Estates General of 1789

Drawing up the lists of complaints created great excitement everywhere in France. So when the Estates General finally met at Versailles in May 1789, millions of people had great expectations of it. It seemed to many people that the king was interested in their problems and that he was going to take action to solve them.

The Estates meet

The first meeting of the Estates General took place on 5 May 1789. Over a thousand deputies met in the largest hall in Versailles. After long speeches by the King and his chief ministers, the three estates were told to split up and carry on the meeting in separate halls.

The third estate deputies were unhappy with this order. By meeting in three separate halls, where each estate had a single vote, they could be outvoted by the clergy and nobility. So they refused to discuss anything as a separate group. They said they would take part in the Estates General only if the nobles and clergy joined them in a single 'National Assembly'.

The nobles and clergy refused to do so. After weeks of argument about the matter, the third estate gave them an ultimatum. If, at the end of a week, the nobles and clergy had not joined them, they would start the work of the Estates General by themselves.

This was an act of defiance against the king. The third estate was refusing to work by his rules for the Estates General. Louis angrily ordered a Royal Session of the Estates General. He intended to warn the third estate not to defy him any further.

Louis, however, was losing control of events at Versailles for, on 19 June, the clergy decided to join the third estate. The following morning, the third estate deputies arrived at the palace to welcome the clergy into their meeting hall. They arrived to find its doors locked and guarded by soldiers. Inside, workmen were preparing it for the king's Royal Session.

35 Louis XVI (top left) presides over the first meeting of the Estates General, 5 May 1789. To his right sit 291 clergy, to his left 270 nobles. Facing him are the 578 deputies of the third estate. Painted by Charles-Auguste Couder in 1839.

The Tennis Court Oath

This angered and excited the deputies of the third estate. They feared that Louis was going to break up their assembly by force. With rain falling, they took shelter in the nearest empty building they could find, a tennis court less than two minutes away. Packed inside the court, they took an oath to carry on meeting until they had changed the way France was governed.

This dramatic oath tied the deputies together in a common cause. So when the king held his Royal Session on 23 June, and ordered them to meet in their separate estates, they refused to move. One of their leaders told him 'We shall only leave at the point of bayonets.'

Louis could have ordered his soldiers to make them leave. But, faced with such determination, he gave in to them. On 27 June he ordered the nobles and clergy to join them in a single assembly. Thus, the National Assembly became France's legal parliament. Cheering crowds let off fireworks when they heard the decision.

To many people at the time, these events seemed like a revolution. An Englishman who witnessed them wrote, 'the whole business now seems over and the revolution complete.' But as you can find out in the next chapter, this 'revolution' was far from complete. It had only just begun.

36 This picture of the Tennis Court Oath, drawn by Jacques-Louis David in 1791, shows all but one of the 578 third-estate deputies, along with seven clergymen from the first estate, swearing to carry on meeting until they had changed the way France was governed. If the weather had been fine on 20 June 1789, how might this picture have been different?

Review and Assessment

1 Study sources 6 (page 7), 12 (page 10), 13 (page 11), 16 (page 14), 20 (page 16), 26 (page 18) and 32 (page 20). Then, on a full page, make a table like the one below. In the boxes on the left, write a sentence about the things that many people disliked about society, tax, feudal rights and dues, law and government. In the boxes on the right, write down which kinds of people were most likely to complain about these things.

	Things that people disliked	Kinds of people who disliked these things
Society (source 5)		
Taxation (source 12)		
Feudal rights and dues (source 13)		
Law (source 16)		
Government (sources 19, 25 and 31)		

2 Look at your completed table. Choose from it at least one reason why many French people wanted to change the way France was run.

3 Sort these events and developments into the order in which they happened:

A an assembly of nobles and clergy refused to agree to the new tax, so . . .

B the government was deeply in debt, so . . .

C Louis XVI ordered a meeting of the Estates General, hoping it would agree to the new tax. But . . .

D the Third Estate deputies took over the Estates General and turned it into a National Assembly, so . . .

E The government spent more each year than it received in taxes, so . . .

F the deputies gathered in a tennis court and swore an oath that they would continue to meet.

G the Finance Minister planned to raise money with a new tax on land. But . . .

H Louis XVI decided to hold a royal session of the Estates General, and warn the third estate not to defy him, but . . .

I the government went bankrupt, so . . .

Which of these events and developments were causes, and which were consequences, of the meeting of the Estates General?

4 Here are some reasons why Louis XVI and his government were unpopular by 1789:

People thought the king and his ministers had too much power (e.g. *lettres de cachet*)

Nobles disliked the government's plans for a new land tax because they would lose their privilege of tax exemption

People disliked Marie Antoinette's extravagent spending

People disliked the fact that Marie Antoinette was Austrian

Many poor people blamed the government for high prices and unemployment

Which of those reasons were mainly a) political, b) social, and c) economic?

5 Which of the reasons for the government's unpopularity (above) do you think was the most important? Explain your answer.

6 If Louis XVI had not married Marie Antoinette, do you think his government would still have been unpopular by 1789? Explain your answer.

2 Revolution and Terror, 1789–1794

The revolution which began at Versailles in 1789 soon spread to other parts of France. Over the next five years, it brought about great changes in the country's society, government and religion. Later, those changes would spread to other countries all over the world.

Because the revolution changed so much, people had strong feelings about it. Many became keen revolutionaries who welcomed the changes. Millions more hated the revolution and did all they could to halt it. This chapter describes the changes that took place and looks at some of the ways in which people viewed them, both at the time and since.

Revolution, 1789

Setting up the National Assembly was a great victory for the third estate but a defeat for the king. Louis XVI had lost control of the Estates General. Riots in nearby Paris showed that he risked losing control of the capital too. Urged on by the queen and members of his court, Louis ordered 20,000 royal troops to move into the area around Paris. He said this was to keep order there, but most people suspected that the troops were going to break up the National Assembly. People in Paris started to feel afraid.

Their fears grew on 12 July. News came from Versailles that Louis had sacked the popular finance minister, Necker, and replaced him with a hard-liner who opposed the third estate. People assumed that Louis was about to crack down on the National Assembly. Angry and frightened crowds started looking for weapons to defend themselves against the king's troops.

1 *Attack on the Bastille*, **painted by Charles Thévenin in 1795.**

The search for weapons went on for two days. Crowds broke into arms stores and stole thousands of guns. On the morning of 14 July rumours went round that there were tonnes of gunpowder in the Bastille, an old fortress in the east end of Paris.

The storming of the Bastille

Parisians hated the Bastille. For hundreds of years it had been a prison where prisoners of the crown were sent by sealed letters (see page 18). Everybody had heard stories about it: of dark, stinking dungeons, of torture chambers, and of masked prisoners chained to the walls for life.

The crowd that now came to the Bastille looking for weapons was full of these tales. The fortress, to them, was a symbol of all they hated about the king's power. They broke into the courtyard and threatened to blow down the gates with cannons. The governor decided to give in but the angry crowd would not hear of surrender. They wanted to destroy this symbol of royal power. When he let down the drawbridge they stormed inside, smashing anything in their way and killing its defenders. By evening, they had control of the Bastille.

2 *A Cell in the Bastille,* **painted by Jean-Pierre Houël in 1789.**

Images of the Bastille

The fall of the Bastille was one of the most famous events of the French Revolution. It was a symbol of the victory of ordinary people over the power of their rulers. Their victory was recorded in many thousands of drawings and paintings. Let us examine the image they created.

Many of the pictures show the dramatic events that led up to the capture of the Bastille. Picture 1 on page 29 shows the climax of events – the arrest of the prison governor, the Marquis de Launay. It was painted by a well-known artist of the time who specialised in painting historical scenes.

Some pictures, like source 2, claimed to show what the attackers found inside the Bastille after they had captured it. Painted by another well-known artist of the time, it shows prisoners chained to the walls of a rat-infested dungeon, one of them wearing an iron mask. The ladder in the foreground suggests there may be more prisoners in another dungeon below.

Copies of pictures like these appeared in their thousands. They were seen all over France, and they created images of the Bastille that everybody could recognise. Foreigners were fascinated by them, and artists abroad produced their own versions of events. Source 3, by a British artist, shows prisoners being helped out of a dungeon. One of the gaolers is pointing to even deeper dungeons beneath.

3 An engraving by James Gillray, *The Triumph of Liberty in the opening of the Bastille*, published on 12 July 1790.

But were these images accurate? If cameras had existed then, could they have filmed such images? According to this account of what the attackers found, written by a leading French historian, the answer must be no:

4 The attackers were astonished to find so few captives. Many believed there were others, hidden in some secret cavern or dungeon . . . On 18 July the four gaolers were questioned separately. They confirmed that the Bastille contained, on 14 July, only seven prisoners: Solages, Whyte, Tavernier, Béchade, La Corrège, Pujade and Laroche. The latter four, common law prisoners accused of forgery, disappeared soon after and were never seen again. The Count of Solages had been imprisoned at the request of his family . . . Whyte was an Englishman, afflicted by madness, and on 15 July he was imprisoned in Charenton. Tavernier was equally mad and he too was sent to Charenton.

Jacques Godechot, *La Prise de la Bastille* [The Storming of the Bastille], 1965

Now try comparing the pictures with another kind of evidence. Sources 5 and 6 are extracts from the diary of a prisoner who was inside the Bastille until a week before it was attacked. One is a list of some of the meals he ate there. The other is an account of his spending for the month of December 1787.

5

Wednesday		Friday	
lunch	soup	lunch	soup
	a veal kidney		a sole
	chocolate cream		rice pudding
	two baked apples		two baked apples
supper	soup	supper	soup
	two coddled eggs		four fresh eggs

Thursday		Saturday	
lunch	soup	lunch	soup
	two partridge wings		two lamb cutlets
	two baked pears		coffee cream
			two baked apples
supper	soup	supper	soup
	minced meat from		omelette with sugar
	the remains of		two eggs in butter
	the partridge		

6

December 1787			livres	sous
2nd	Paid to Lenoble, tailor		1	5
4th	4 pounds of candles		2	12
	Bottle of elixir of Garus		1	10
	Bottle of brandy			16
5th	For having a tie darned			4
	A pound of sugar		1	2
6th	18 cut quills			18
8th	Pot of apricot jam		1	16
11th	. . . a pair of scissors		3	0
14th	Bottle of Alicante wine		3	5
	Two bottles of wine			8
	Half a box of nails			3
16th	Pot of apricot jam		1	16
17th	18 cut quills			18
19th	Re-soling a pair of shoes		2	5
20th	A bound notebook		2	0
21st	Three packets of writing paper			10
22nd	A pair of shoes		6	0
	Two pounds of powder, two jars of pommade,		1	18
	and scent			
23rd	Two pounds of candles		6	8
25th	8 cut quills			18

Marquis de Sade, *Letters and Miscellaneous Writings from Vincennes and the Bastille*, 1777–89

1 **Using sources 2 and 3 as evidence, describe what it was like to be a prisoner in the Bastille.**

2 **How do sources 4, 5 and 6 disagree with the image of the Bastille created by sources 2 and 3?**

3 **Source 3 was painted a year after the event, by which time it was well known that such things had not been found in the Bastille.**

Why do you think the artist painted a picture of events he must have known did not happen?

The king loses control

Louis XVI considered sending his army into Paris to recapture the Bastille. His war minister, however, warned him that the soldiers would probably refuse orders to do so. Louis therefore had to give up control of Paris. He ordered his army back to its barracks. To keep order in Paris he allowed the people to set up their own military force, the National Guard. To run the city, leading officials of the third estate formed a new local government, the Paris Commune.

Towns and cities all over France followed the example of Paris. Rioting crowds attacked town halls, forced out the royal officials, and set up their own communes and National Guard units.

7 **Nobles flee from the countryside while peasants attack and burn their castles. A popular print of 1789.**

The Great Fear

The violence then spread into the countryside, where unemployment was high and millions were hungry. Many thousands of people had left home to seek work or to beg, and were now wandering around the countryside looking for food. Farmers lived in fear of gangs of wanderers who stole food from their fields and damaged their farms.

As harvest time approached, rumours swept the countryside that nobles were trying to starve the people by hoarding grain. The rumours also said that nobles were paying the gangs of wanderers to attack farms and terrorise the peasants. Angry peasants responded to the rumours by refusing to pay their feudal dues. In many places they broke into their lords' homes and burned records of their dues.

As the violence spread, fear of gangs increased. Villagers who thought they saw gangs rang the church bells to warn neighbouring villages. The warnings, passed from town to town, spread the panic to many parts of France. By late July, the whole country was gripped by a 'Great Fear'.

The Assembly begins its work

The deputies in the National Assembly were scared by the violence of the peasants. They took drastic measures to end it. On the night of 4 August, noble deputies, one by one, announced that they would give up their feudal rights and dues. By the next morning hunting rights, tithes, the *corvée*, and the rights of the mill and the oven had all been abolished. Feudalism was dead.

Three weeks later, the Assembly made another important change to French society. It issued a 'Declaration of the Rights of Man and the Citizen'. This stated that all men were free and equal in rights. It said people should have the right to speak and write freely. It changed the laws of arrest and imprisonment, and banned torture. Above all, it said that power in France belonged to the entire people, not just the king.

8 Some of the women and National Guardsmen who took the Royal Family back to Paris.

The women march to Versailles

Louis XVI disliked these decisions of the Assembly. He refused to sign them, which meant they could not become law. Then, early in October, he brought more soldiers to Versailles to add to his bodyguard. Again it looked as if he was going to break up the Assembly by armed force.

When news of this reached Paris, crowds of market women gathered in the streets. They marched through the city, collecting weapons. On 5 October, armed with knives, sticks, rifles and two cannons, they marched to Versailles to protest. Supported by National Guardsmen, they complained to the king about the high price of bread and about the extra soldiers in Versailles. They asked him to leave Versailles and come with them to live in Paris. This would allow them to keep an eye on his activities.

Louis did not want to go. He changed his mind when a group of the women smashed their way into his palace, killed two bodyguards and threatened to kill the queen. On 6 October Louis, Marie Antoinette and their oldest son travelled in a coach to Paris, surrounded by a crowd of 60,000 people. The Palace of Versailles was locked and boarded up. From then on they lived in the Tuileries Palace in the centre of Paris.

1 The women in source 8 are carrying branches of laurel leaves to show they have won a victory. In what way were the events of 5–6 October a victory for the women of Paris?

The King and the Assembly, 1789–1792

Reforms of the National Assembly

The deputies of the National Assembly followed the royal family to Paris, where they took over an old riding school as a meeting place. Over the next two years the Assembly made many new laws, changing the way France was organised and run. Source 9 below shows the most important of those reforms.

9 **Reforms of the National Assembly**

1. Male tax-payers over 25 years old were given the right to vote.
2. All Church land was confiscated so that it could be sold to pay France's debts.
3. The Assembly paid off France's debts with bank notes called *assignats*: people who were owed money were given *assignats* with which they could buy confiscated church land.
4. Local government was re-organised. Local councils were elected by citizens.
5. Protestants were given the same voting rights as Catholics.
6. France was divided into 83 Departments, each run by an elected council.
7. Jews were given the same voting rights as everyone else.
8. The salt tax (*gabelle*) was abolished.
9. Most monasteries and convents were closed down.
10. *Assignats* became France's legal currency.
11. Noble titles were abolished.
12. The Church was reformed: a 'Civil Constitution of the Clergy' said that bishops and priests must be elected by the people and must take an oath of loyalty to France.
13. A new system of law courts was created. Judges were to be elected by citizens.
14. The *traites* taxes were abolished.
15. A tax on land was introduced.
16. Trade guilds were abolished.
17. The *aides* taxes were abolished.
18. The *taille* tax was abolished.
19. Black people in French colonies were given the same rights as white people.
20. Slavery in France was abolished.
21. The Assembly introduced a constitution* describing how France would be governed.

* constitution: a set of rules describing how an organisation or a country should be run.

2 By number, put the reforms of the Assembly into the following categories: political reforms, financial reforms, social reforms, religious reforms. Which kind of reform seems to have been most important?

10 *Abuses of the religious orders*: an engraving of 1789 shows monks leading unholy lives when they are not in church.

1 Look at source 10. What point do you think the artist was trying to make?

The reform of the Church

Most people welcomed these reforms. On one issue, however, they were divided. That was the reform of the Church. On one side of the argument were growing numbers of people who thought the Church had too much power, too much land and too much money. They also thought that many of the clergy lived unholy lives. Their point of view can be seen in the imaginary picture of a monastery above. On the other side were millions of God-fearing Catholics who had never questioned the way the Church was run, and who could see no reason to change it.

So when the National Assembly began to take land and money from the Church, many Catholics protested. Their protests grew louder in July 1790 when the Assembly drew up a law reducing the power of the Church. The law, called the Civil Constitution of the Clergy, said that priests and bishops must be elected like other public officials. It ordered all clergy to take an oath of loyalty to the French nation and the law.

Over half the clergy refused to take this oath. They said that the Assembly had no right to interfere in Church affairs. The Pope supported their protest by condemning the new law. From then on, the clergy were divided between those who took the oath and who supported the revolution, and those who refused the oath and opposed the revolution. Millions of people followed the examples set by their priests. Before long, therefore, the entire nation was divided by the question of the Church and its power.

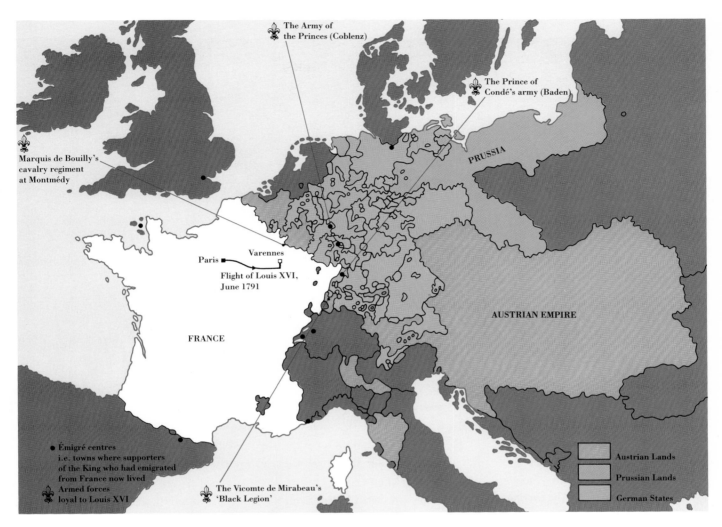

The Army of
the Princes (Coblenz)

The Prince of
Condé's army (Baden)

PRUSSIA

Marquis de Bouilly's
cavalry regiment
at Montmédy

Paris   Varennes

Flight of Louis XVI,
June 1791

FRANCE

AUSTRIAN EMPIRE

● Émigré centres
  i.e. towns where supporters
  of the King who had emigrated
  from France now lived
  Armed forces
  loyal to Louis XVI

The Vicomte de Mirabeau's
'Black Legion'

Austrian Lands

Prussian Lands

German States

The flight to Varennes

Louis XVI was deeply unhappy with the Civil Constitution. He sided with the priests who refused to take the oath. This made it look, yet again, as if he opposed the revolution. Angry crowds protested at the gates of the Tuileries Palace.

Urged on by his wife and by members of his court, Louis now decided to leave France. Their aim was to get help from the French princes who had already left France and had built up armies just across the frontier (see the map above). They also hoped for assistance from Marie Antoinette's brother Leopold, the Emperor of Austria. They would then be able to invade France, get rid of the Assembly, and take back the power they had lost.

Leaving France, however, was far from easy. Because the Assembly suspected that Louis might try to escape, there were guards at every door in the Palace. Louis and his family therefore had to make a secret escape.

Close to midnight on 21 June 1791, Louis, Antoinette and their children, all in disguise, crept out of the palace through a temporarily unguarded door.

11 **The armies of the princes and the flight of the royal family, June 1791.**

Study the map carefully:
2 **Suggest why Louis tried escaping eastwards instead of heading north or south.**
3 **Judging by the map, why might Louis have thought the Austrian Emperor would be able to help him invade France?**

12 A painting by Laurent Guyot shows the royal family in their coach being arrested at Varennes. Stones are being placed under the carriage wheels to prevent any attempt at escape.

A waiting carriage then took them eastwards towards Montmédy, close to the frontier 250 km away.

They were still 50 km from the frontier when they were recognised. News of their escape was sent ahead and the local authorities were waiting for them in the little town of Varennes. They were arrested and sent back to Paris the next day. As they went, crowds shouted insults and spat at the windows.

The road to war

The flight to Varennes was the first step on a road to war. Believing that Louis and Antoinette were now in danger, Emperor Leopold issued a statement promising to help them regain their liberty and their power. Then, with the King of Prussia, he called on all European kings to take action to help Louis.

Leopold privately had no intention of attacking France. His statement was just a show of support for a fellow monarch and for his sister. But nobody in France knew that. Rumours flew about that foreign armies, along with the armies of the French princes, would soon invade. Before long, most people were convinced that war was inevitable.

Far from fearing war, many French people wanted it. Louis and his supporters wanted war because they expected the French armies to lose it. Then Louis could be restored to power. People who opposed Louis wanted war

13 *Sacrifice to the Nation*, a painting of 1801 by Julien Delarue, shows a French volunteer leaving home to fight in the army. Pinned on the wall is the Assembly's declaration 'Citoyens, La Patrie est en Danger' (Citizens, the Fatherland is in danger).

because they thought it would force him to show exactly whose side he was on. If he took the side of the invaders, they would then be able to de-throne him and make France a Republic – a country in which the people hold power through an assembly and a president who they elect.

War

War began on 20 April 1792 when France declared war on Austria. Hoping for a quick win, the French armies attacked Austrian bases across the frontier in Belgium. But the Austrians were better organised, better equipped and better led. They easily beat off the French attack.

In Paris, people blamed the French defeat on traitors. Rumours flew around that there was an 'Austrian Committee' in the Tuileries Palace, passing France's military secrets to the the Austrians. People grew afraid. Their fears increased when Prussia joined forces with Austria in May.

The Assembly took emergency measures to deal with this threat. It ordered every soldier in Paris to the frontier. It put a watch on all foreigners. It decided that priests who still refused to take an oath of loyalty should be expelled from the country. And, on 11 July, it declared that 'The Fatherland is in Danger' and appealed to all citizens to volunteer for the army. Source 13 shows just one of the volunteers who answered the Assembly's appeal.

Look at source 13.
1 According to this painting, what was the volunteer sacrificing by going to serve in the army?
2 Judging by how he painted the scene, what do you think the artist wanted us to think about the volunteer?

Such measures put Louis into a difficult position. He disagreed especially with the measure against priests. This angered his opponents. 20,000 of them showed their anger by breaking into the Tuileries on 20 June and shouting abuse at him.

Louis' position became more difficult in July. The enemy commander, the Duke of Brunswick, issued a statement known as the Brunswick Manifesto. It threatened the people of Paris with terrible punishments if Louis was harmed in any way.

Far from protecting Louis and his family, the Brunswick Manifesto put them in great danger. When news of it reached Paris, the Assembly ordered weapons to be given to all citizens so that they could defend themselves. But now that they had weapons, the people of Paris could do whatever they wanted. Above all, they wanted to get rid of the monarchy and to set up a new kind of assembly in which they had power.

14 **The storming of the Tuileries on 10 August 1792. A painting by Jean Bertaux shows Parisians, backed by National Guards, fighting the red-uniformed Swiss Guards.**

The storming of the Tuileries

On 10 August 1792, 20,000 armed men and women marched to the Tuileries, determined to de-throne Louis XVI. Source 14 shows some of the things that happened when they got there. Helped by National Guards (in blue uniforms) they broke into the palace grounds. The red-uniformed Swiss Guards, defending the king, tried to fight them off but were outnumbered. They retreated, but the attackers caught up with them. Using knives, pikes and axes they slaughtered 600 of the Swiss Guards. Many of the attackers mutilated the dead bodies. Later, as the picture below shows, they ransacked the palace.

The overthrow of the monarchy

The attack on the Tuileries led quickly to the end of the monarchy. Louis was suspended from office and, with his family, was imprisoned. A new assembly

What impression does picture 15 give of the people who stormed the Tuileries? What impression is created by picture 14?

15 Plundering the king's cellars, 10 August 1792. A painting of 1795 by Johann Zoffany shows Parisians stealing wine from the Tuileries.

called the Convention was set up as the country's new law-making body. Its first action, on 21 September 1792, was to de-throne Louis and declare that France was now a Republic. Two months later it put him on trial for high treason. It found him guilty and sentenced him to death. He was beheaded in public on 21 January 1793.

The *sans culottes*

The people who overthrew the king called themselves *sans culottes*. They were the working people of Paris, ranging from craftsmen to laundry women, clerks to porters, fishwives to labourers. Although they varied in the work they did and the money they earned, they had many ideas in common and behaved in similar ways.

Sans culottes hated nobles. The men wore trousers rather than the knee breeches (culottes) that nobles wore. They refused to use any word that had noble connections. So, instead of calling each other *monsieur* (literally, 'my lord') or *madame* ('my lady') they addressed each other as 'Citizen' or 'Comrade'.

16 This cartoon by James Gillray was published in Britain two weeks after the September Massacres of 1792, when *sans culottes* hacked to death some 1,400 inmates of the prisons in Paris.

Sans culottes were Republicans, which meant they hated the monarchy and thought power should belong to ordinary people like themselves. Many re-named themselves or called their children after famous Republicans of the past – Brutus or William Tell, for example.

Sans culottes believed very strongly that everyone should have equal rights, such as the right to vote. To show that nobody was superior to anyone else they used the familiar '*tu*' for 'you' when they spoke to people rather than '*vous*', which was the usual way of addressing people outside the family.

Finally, *sans culottes* claimed the right to carry weapons and to use them against their opponents. In September 1792, for example, they broke into the prisons of Paris and murdered around 1,400 prisoners whom they suspected of supporting the Austrians.

Their readiness to use violence horrified foreigners. Source 16, by the British cartoonist James Gillray, shows what many British people thought of the *sans culottes*. Compare it with source 17 by a French painter.

The war spreads

The execution of Louis XVI shocked millions of people all over Europe. Louis' fellow monarchs were outraged. One by one, in the first months of 1793, they joined forces with Austria and Prussia in their war against France. The aim of this coalition, or alliance, was to destroy the new French Republic.

Far from scaring the revolutionaries in France, this made them more war-like than before. They wanted to fight these 'tyrants', as they called all kings, and spread the revolution to the rest of Europe. Rather than wait for the coalition to attack them, they declared war on its three latest members – Britain, Holland and Spain. France was now at war with most of Europe.

Disaster immediately struck the French armies. Austrian forces beat them in a series of battles in the Netherlands. The French commander, General Dumouriez, abandoned his men and went over to the Austrian side. France seemed on the verge of defeat.

Inflation and shortages

The war was only one of many difficulties facing the new government. A major problem was the high price of food. Prices were rising because, to pay for the war, the government was printing huge amounts of paper money called *assignats* (see page 35). But the more bank notes it printed, the less they were worth: the currency was suffering from inflation. By February 1793 a bank note was worth only half the amount printed on it.

As well as being expensive, bread was also scarce because farmers did not want to sell their grain for bank notes that were losing their value. Hungry *sans culottes* began raiding shops and food stores to get the food they could not buy.

17 Portrait of an actor dressed as a *sans culotte*, painted by Louis-Léopold Boilly in October 1792.

1 What did a) Louis-Léopold Boilly (picture 17) and b) James Gillray (picture 16) want us to think about the *sans culottes*?

2 Do you think either of these pictures can be trusted as an accurate picture of the *sans culottes*? Explain your answer.

1 Judging by the map, what chance did the revolutionary government have of surviving the crisis of 1793? Explain your answer.

Rebellion

A third major problem hit the government when, to defend the country, it ordered an extra 300,000 men to join the armies. This order was deeply unpopular. In the Vendée in western France, where many people were royalists, thousands of peasants joined in an armed rebellion against the government.

In Paris, the war led to a conflict between two groups of politicians in the Convention: the Girondins, who held most of the important posts in the government, and the Jacobins, who were supported by the *sans culottes*. The Jacobins blamed the Girondins for France's defeats on the battlefield, and for allowing food prices to rise. On 2 June an angry crowd of *sans culottes* broke into the Convention and expelled the leading Girondins.

This triggered off a string of revolts in the provinces which supported the Girondins. By summer 1793, sixty out of eighty-three departments had joined the rebellion against the government.

18 The crisis of 1793.

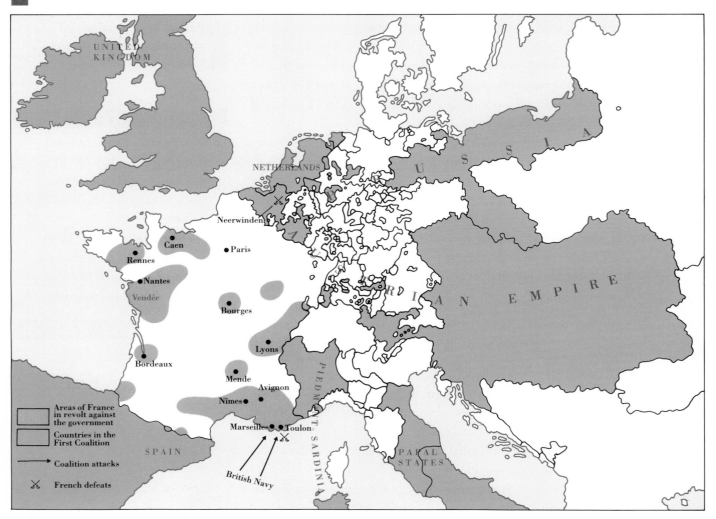

The Reign of Terror

Faced with all these disasters, the Convention set up an emergency group called the Committee of Public Safety. Its twelve members had the power to do anything they thought necessary to save France. For the next twelve months they used this power to run France very strictly and to impose harsh punishments on opponents. So harsh was the Committee's rule that it was known as the 'Reign of Terror'.

The Law of Suspects

The Terror began with a 'Law of Suspects' in September 1793. Groups of citizens in every town had to draw up lists of people they suspected of opposing the government. Almost anyone could fall under suspicion. The Law said that suspects were people who 'by their behaviour, their contacts, their words or their writings, showed themselves to be . . . enemies of Liberty.' In the year that followed, over a quarter of a million suspects were arrested and put in prison.

Many suspects were sent to Paris for trial by the Revolutionary Tribunal. This was a special court set up to deal with political offences. Its judges could impose sentences of imprisonment, deportation or death. Around half the sentences they passed were death sentences.

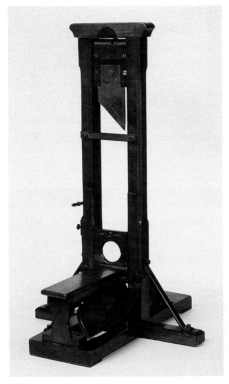

19 A model of the type of guillotine used during the Reign of Terror.

The guillotine

Death sentences were carried out by beheading prisoners with a recently invented machine. Known as a guillotine after the person who first suggested using it, Doctor Guillotin, it was meant to be quicker and less painful than the methods of execution used before the Revolution (see page 14). An English journalist described how it worked:

20 He [the prisoner] is first tied to a plank of wood of about eighteen inches [45cm] broad, and an inch [2.5cm] thick, with cords about the arms, body and legs; this plank is about four feet [1.2m] long, and comes almost up to the chin; the executioner then lays him on his belly on the bench, lifts up the upper part of the board which receives his neck, inserts his head, then shuts the board and pulls the string fastened to a peg at the top of the machine, which lifts up a catch. The axe falls down, and the head, which is off in an instant, is received in a basket ready for that purpose, as is the body in another basket.

From an anonymous broadsheet, *Massacre of the French King*, 1793

Around 17,000 suspects were executed by guillotine during the Terror. One of the first to die was Marie Antoinette, executed in October 1793 for treason.

2 Compare sources 19 and 20 with the picture on page 14. Do you agree that the guillotine was a humane form of execution?

21 Four sisters and their mother waiting their turn to be guillotined in Nantes on 18 December 1793. They were arrested as suspects because they were relations of one of the rebel leaders in the Vendée. *Sans culottes* look on in horror as they pray together at the foot of the scaffold.

1 Suggest what the artist wanted us to think about the women.

2 Where do you think the artist's sympathies lay – with the women or with the *sans culottes*? Explain your answer.

Terror in the provinces

The Committee of Public Safety took very strong measures to crush the revolts in the countryside. Over a hundred Representatives of the Convention were sent to the provinces with instructions to do anything necessary to restore order. In the Vendée, where the biggest revolt was taking place, the Representative on Mission was Jean-Baptiste Carrier. When the guillotine proved too slow to execute captured rebels, he had them drowned in boat-loads in the River Loire. At least 2,000 died in these drownings at Nantes. In Lyons, nearly 2,000 rebels were executed. To speed up the executions, prisoners were lined up in front of open graves and blasted into them with cannon fire.

Terror in the armies

In August 1793 the Convention ordered a 'Mass Levy' of the French people. This meant that every citizen had to take an active part in the war effort. Unmarried men had to join the armies to fight. Married men were to make weapons for them. Women were to make tents and serve in hospitals. Children were to make bandages and gunpowder.

The Mass Levy increased the French armies to 800,000 men, nearly three times the size of the Coalition's armies. Representatives of the Convention made sure that strict discipline was kept. Generals who did not win battles were replaced by younger officers who had proved their ability in action.

Economic Terror

The Committee tried to halt the rise in food prices with a Law of the Maximum in September 1793. This said that the prices of forty goods, such as corn, flour, firewood and oil, must stay fixed until further notice. So too must people's wages. Breaking the Maximum carried the death penalty.

22 **The impact of the Terror.**

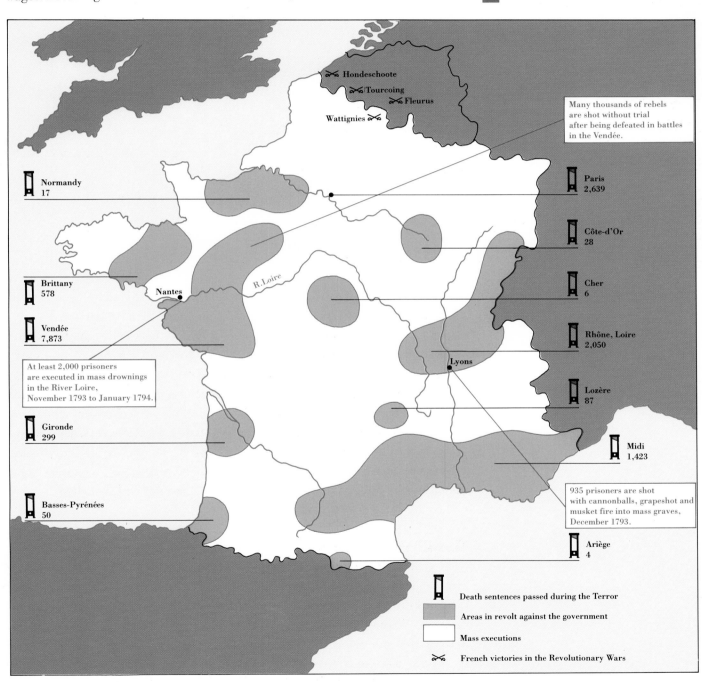

Many thousands of rebels are shot without trial after being defeated in battles in the Vendée.

Hondeschoote

Tourcoing

Fleurus

Wattignies

Normandy
17

Paris
2,639

Côte-d'Or
28

Brittany
578

Nantes

Cher
6

Vendée
7,873

R. Loire

Rhône, Loire
2,050

Lyons

At least 2,000 prisoners are executed in mass drownings in the River Loire, November 1793 to January 1794.

Lozère
87

Gironde
299

Midi
1,423

935 prisoners are shot with cannonballs, grapeshot and musket fire into mass graves, December 1793.

Basses-Pyrénées
50

Ariège
4

Death sentences passed during the Terror

Areas in revolt against the government

Mass executions

French victories in the Revolutionary Wars

23 The Revolutionary Calendar. This one had moving windows.

1 If this calendar was still in use today, what year would this be?
2 When is your birthday in the Revolutionary Calendar?
3 Most French people hated the new calendar. Suggest why.

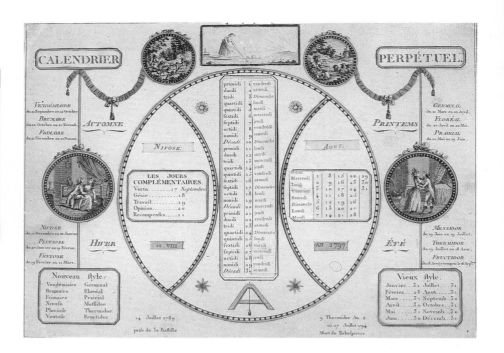

Terror and the Church

The Terror led to the disappearance of the Christian religion in many parts of France. Claiming that Christianity was no more than 'superstition', *sans culottes* closed down churches, robbed them of their bells and silver, and sacked their priests. In many towns, a 'Cult of Reason', based on revolutionary ideas such as Liberty, took the place of Christianity.

As part of the campaign against Christianity, the Convention introduced a new calendar. Years were no longer counted from the birth of Christ but from September 1792, when the Republic was founded. 1792–3 was re-named Year One, so the Terror took place in Year Two. Each year was divided into twelve thirty-day months with names describing their weather or growing seasons. Months were divided into three ten-day weeks. Sunday was abolished.

Results of the Terror

The Committee of Public Safety achieved what it set out to do. It saved France from collapse. By mid 1794 the French armies had driven their enemies right out of France and had occupied the Austrian Netherlands. The Representatives on Mission had crushed all the revolts in the Provinces. And although prices were still rising, the Committee had managed to avoid a famine.

The price of success had been high. Between 35,000 and 40,000 people had been executed or had died in filthy, overcrowded prisons. Everybody's rights and freedoms had been severely limited. Prices were still rising. And the Committee had became a kind of twelve-man dictatorship.

The coup of Thermidor

By the summer of 1794 the Committee was very unpopular. Many deputies in the Convention disliked it because they thought it was too powerful. Some disliked it because they feared ending up under the guillotine. Others disliked it because they could not see any need for the Terror now that the revolts were over and France was winning the war. Even the *sans culottes*, its strongest supporters, were unhappy because their wages were held down by the Maximum law, while prices were still rising.

On 27 July 1794–9 Thermidor, Year Two in the new calendar – the Convention decided to get rid of the Committee's leading member, Robespierre , along with his supporters. Twenty-one were arrested and guillotined the following day. A further ninety-six were executed the day after.

With Robespierre dead, the Convention reduced the power of the Committee, freed hundreds of suspects, abolished the Maximum and got rid of the Revolutionary Tribunal. The Terror thus came to an end.

24 *The Night of the 9–10 of Thermidor, Year Two*, by J.J. Tassaert, shows Robespierre and his supporters being arrested by soldiers sent by the Convention. The artist shows Robespierre being shot in the jaw by one of the soldiers, but most historians write that he actually shot himself in a failed attempt to commit suicide.

Review and Assessment

25 *Monument to the Glory of Louis XVI engraved by Vincenzio Vangelisti in 1789.*

1 Look carefully at source 25. It is an engraving made in the summer of 1789 and presented as a gift to Louis XVI. It shows Louis standing on a pedestal marked 'father of the nation, king of a free people'. With him on the pedestal are the goddesses of truth and justice. On the right, the queen listens to the grievances of the people. On the left, an angel destroys the 'feudal system'.

a What happened in 1789 to make the French 'a free people'?

b What was 'the feudal system' and how was it destroyed in 1789?

c What is justice? In what ways did 'justice' triumph in 1789?

2 Source 25 is an imaginary picture based on events that actually happened and people who really lived. Find two people in the picture who really lived and two who are imaginary.

3 Now look carefully at source 26. It is the same engraving with changes made ten years later. The artist has replaced Louis with the goddess of Liberty and the queen with a woman representing the French nation. You should be able to spot several other differences between the two pictures.

a Make a list of differences between pictures 25 and 26.

b Suggest why the artist made these changes.

26 *Liberty Triumphant.* The same engraving as that in source 25 with modifications made in 1800.

4 After Louis XVI was overthrown there was a 'Reign of Terror' in which everybody's rights and freedoms were severely limited. Yet, in picture 26, the artist suggests that people had more freedom after Louis had been overthrown. What reasons might the artist have had for suggesting this?

5
a Which of the following statements about France after 1792 might the artist of source 26 have used to support his point of view?

b Which of the statements could be used to disagree with the artist's point of view?

A All French citizens had the right to vote.

B All citizens had to take an active part in the war.

C 250,000 people were imprisoned by the Law of Suspects.

D A new calendar with a ten-day week was used to keep time.

E The Christian religion was replaced by a Cult of Reason based on the ideas of liberty and equality.

F The Maximum law banned price and wage rises.

G France was governed by a Convention elected by all citizens.

H Aristocrats were no longer superior to everyone else in society.

I 17,000 people were guillotined as enemies of the Republic.

J France fought and won a war against a coalition of seven countries.

6 Judging by your answers to question 5, how far do you agree with the artist's interpretation of the events of the Revolution?

3 The rise of Napoleon

After the Terror ended, the French tried a new form of government. From 1795 to 1799 they were governed by five men called the Directors, backed by two new assemblies called Councils. They did not govern France well. Prices shot up, money lost all its value and many people starved. In 1799 a young army general forced them out of office and took over the government. His name was Napoleon Bonaparte. This chapter describes how he rose to power.

Napoleon the soldier

Napoleon's background

Napoleon was born on the island of Corsica in 1769 (see the map on page 54). He was the second of eight children. Just a year earlier, the king of France had bought the island from its Italian owners, so Napoleon was born French while his parents were Italian.

At the age of nine, Napoleon was sent to school in France. He spent the next seven years in military schools, leaving at sixteen as a lieutenant in the French army. Four years later the Revolution began. As the army grew in size during the Revolutionary war, Napoleon gained rapid promotion. He was a general by the age of twenty-four.

Napoleon's brilliant career was nearly wrecked in 1794. He was a close friend of Robespierre's brother Augustin. When Robespierre was overthrown, he was arrested along with everyone else close to the Robespierre brothers. However, the authorities could find no evidence to use against him and had to allow him to return to his army post.

A crucial battle in the Italian campaign: the Battle of Rivoli on 15 January 1797. This picture, painted in 1845 by Félix Philippoteaux, shows Napoleon being helped onto a new horse after his own horse had been shot from under him.

Napoleon's Italian campaign

When the Directors took power in 1795 they continued the Revolutionary war against the Coalition. The French armies by this time were very large, and they quickly conquered Holland and Belgium. Their next targets were the states of northern Italy. This gave Napoleon his next promotion. In 1796 he was made commander of the Army of Italy, with orders to attack Austrian forces in northern Italy.

Over the next eighteen months, Napoleon led his armies in a series of brilliant victories over the Austrians in Italy. By October 1797 all of northern Italy was under French control, and Napoleon was France's most famous general.

Napoleon in Egypt

Following his outstanding success in Italy, the Directors put Napoleon in command of an 'Army of the East'. His orders were to attack Britain's trade and colonies in the Far East. He began by invading Egypt, half way on the trade route to India.

Napoleon quickly defeated the Egyptians at the Battle of the Pyramids in July 1798, but he never got to India. Only a week after the battle, the ships which had brought his army to Egypt were sunk by the British Royal Navy at Aboukir Bay, stranding them in Egypt. They could not advance to India, nor could they return to France.

Napoleon and his army were marooned in the Middle East for a whole year. Back in Europe, unknown to him, the other French armies were faring badly. France's enemies had formed a Second Coalition and had driven them out of Italy and central Europe.

> **Judging by the map below, what made the Second Coalition a dangerous threat to France?**

2 Napoleon's campaigns, 1796–1802.

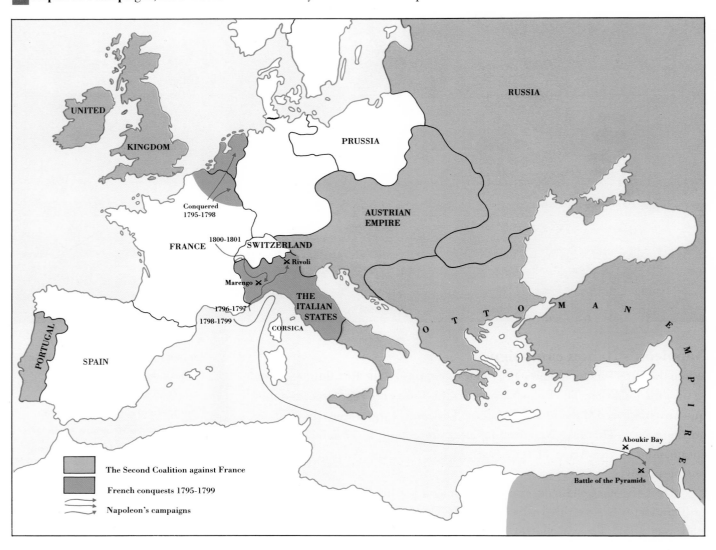

Key:
- The Second Coalition against France
- French conquests 1795-1799
- Napoleon's campaigns

Napoleon learned of these defeats in the summer of 1799. He also learned that rebels had over-run large parts of western France, that the country was nearly bankrupt, and that the Directors were facing strong opposition in the Councils. Although he had no orders to do so, Napoleon left his army in Egypt and hurried back to France. His intention was to save the country from defeat.

Napoleon seizes power

Meanwhile, one of the Directors was plotting to get rid of his fellow Directors, close down the Councils, and set up a new, stronger government. To succeed, he needed military backing. He asked Napoleon to provide it.

Napoleon agreed and joined the plot, along with another of the Directors. Napoleon's brother Lucien, who was President of one of the Councils, was also involved. On 9 November 1799, they took action. They made up a story that rebels were about to capture Paris, and asked the Councils to take emergency action. The Councils did as they were asked and made Napoleon commander of all the troops in the Paris district. Then they left Paris for a safer meeting place in nearby Saint-Cloud. Soldiers then forced the other three Directors to resign.

The next day, Napoleon went to the Councils to ask them to change the government. By this time, however, they had discovered that the story about rebels was a lie. They immediately took an oath to defend the Directory. When Napoleon appeared before them, they shouted at him, pushed him around and tried to declare him an outlaw. According to the Council's own records, angry deputies tried to kill him:

> **3** Some of the deputies shouted out 'kill! kill!' They rushed forward trying to grab him, some armed with pistols and knives. The grenadier guards rushed in to find out why there was such a frightful noise, and shielded him from the killers with their bodies.
>
> From the official record of the Council of Five Hundred, 10 November 1799

Several eye-witnesses reported that one guard was stabbed in the arm while defending Napoleon. But one of the deputies, in his own record of what happened, wrote that:

> **4** I saw the general [Napoleon] escorted by two grenadiers. He was pale-faced, gloomy, his head slightly bent. All I know is that he and his guards were very close to me and that I saw neither guns nor knives raised against him.
>
> Louis-Jacques Savary, *My Self-Examination of the Events of 18 Brumaire Year VIII*

And another deputy later claimed that:

5 The murder attempt on general Bonaparte was a story made up to justify the outrage committed by armed force on the Council. The next day . . . Grenadier Thome told us in a light-hearted manner that he had been summoned to see the general [Napoleon] and that he had been told he had saved the general's life by receiving the dagger blow that was meant for him; that he would be given a pension and made an officer. He added, laughing, that it had been a piece of good luck for him to have torn the sleeve of his coat going through a door.

Dupont de l'Eure, former Deputy of the Council of Five Hundred, writing in 1819

1 **Read source 3. How does this version of events differ from the scene in source 6?**
2 **How do sources 4 and 5 suggest that source 3 is untrue?**
3 **Source 3 comes from the Council's official record of events. Does this mean it can be trusted more than sources 4 and 5?**
4 **According to source 5 why did Napoleon and his supporters make up the story about knives?**

6 Council deputies in their red robes shout 'tyrant!' and 'dictator!' as Napoleon enters their meeting hall. Grenadier guards in bearskin hats protect him. A painting of 1845 by François Bouchot.

Whether it was true or not, the soldiers waiting outside the hall believed that Napoleon's life was in danger. They entered the hall to save him. Most of the deputies fled when they saw the soldiers, many jumping from the windows. A handful who stayed voted to give Napoleon and two of the other plotters the power to run the country until a new type of government could be formed.

Napoleon the ruler

The Consulate

It took only a month to create a new government. France was to be governed by three Consuls, with only the First Consul having the power to make decisions. The other two Consuls were to advise him. Napoleon took the post of First Consul and thus became the head of the government.

To share the work of governing France, four new Councils were created. The most powerful, the Council of State, helped to write new laws and discussed Napoleon's decisions. A Senate, a Tribunate and a Legislative Body also shared in the making of laws and the appointment of officials. In the provinces, officials called Prefects put the laws into effect.

France's 9 million voters were then given the chance to show by voting whether or not they liked this new government. 3 million voted in favour and only 1,500 against. Although 6 million did not bother to vote, Napoleon said that the result showed that the people supported him.

Victory in war

Napoleon's most urgent task as First Consul was to defend France against the armies of the Second Coalition. He planned to do so with an attack on Austrian forces in north Italy. Hoping to surprise them by attacking them from behind, he took his army through Switzerland and across the Alps.

This was a dangerous gamble, and it nearly failed. It took much longer to cross the Alps than Napoleon expected. When his army reached Italy the Austrians were ready for him. They attacked near a village called Marengo. Napoleon's men were outnumbered and exhausted after their long march. They were on the point of defeat when reserve troops unexpectedly arrived on the battlefield and drove the Austrians back. The Battle of Marengo ended in victory for the French.

The defeated Austrians abandoned north Italy. Later that year, another French army defeated the Austrians at the Battle of Hohenlinden in Germany. This brought the war of the Second Coalition to an end. A peace treaty, signed at Lunéville in 1801, left France in control of Belgium, of German lands on the river Rhine, and of north Italy.

7 The Battle of Marengo painted in 1801 by General Lejeune, an amateur artist who was an officer in Napoleon's army.

Can you find Napoleon in this picture? What makes you think it is him?

The making of a legend

Napoleon's victory in the war made him more famous than ever. In newspapers, books and paintings like the one above he was portrayed as a great hero. Before long, Napoleon had become almost a legendary figure.

How much substance was there in the legend? Look at source 9 on page 60. It is one of the most famous of all paintings of Napoleon. It shows him with his army crossing the Great Saint-Bernard pass across the Alps, on his way to fight the Austrians in north Italy.

A leading art historian has explained how Jacques-Louis David painted this portrait:

8 When David proposed to paint him sword in hand, Napoleon . . . replied that battles were no longer won with the sword and that he wished to be painted 'calm, on a fiery horse'. Nor could he see any point in sitting for his likeness . . . to be taken. When David protested that contemporaries must be able to recognise him, Napoleon preferred to think . . . it was only necessary for David to capture a certain idea of genius, not an exact replica of his face.

Anita Brookner, *Jacques-Louis David*, 1980

David could not therefore paint Napoleon from real life. Even so, as another art historian has explained, he made every effort to paint a realistic scene:

10 He asked Constant, the First Consul's valet, to bring the uniform that Napoleon had worn at Marengo, complete with sword, boots and hat, and dressed a dummy in them.

Antoine Schnapper, *David*, 1980

9 **Opposite page. Napoleon crossing the Saint-Bernard, painted in 1800 by Jacques-Louis David.**

11 ***General Bonaparte crossing the Alps*, painted in 1837 by Paul Delaroche.**

But did this mean that David painted a realistic scene? If cameras had existed then, could a photographer have taken such a picture? An answer to that question can be found in Napoleon's own description of how he crossed the Alps:

 The whole army passed the Saint-Bernard on 17, 18, 19 and 20 May. I myself crossed on the 20th; in the most difficult places I rode a mule . . . My guide was a tall robust youth of twenty-two . . .

Napoleon Bonaparte, *Mémoires*, 1823

Fourteen years after Napoleon's memoirs had been published, another French artist painted the same scene (source 11, page 61). You can judge for yourself whether it is more realistic than source 9.

The Concordat and the Catholic Church

Now that France was at peace, Napoleon could deal with some urgent problems. The most difficult of these concerned the Catholic religion. During the Terror, churches had been closed and France was 'de-christianised' (see page 48). Millions of loyal Catholics hated this. In western France, many became rebels, trying to overthrow the government.

Napoleon had to end this religious conflict if his new government was to last. He began by dropping the ten-day week of the Revolutionary Calendar and allowed people to take Sundays off. He told rebel leaders that he would deal with their religious complaints. Most important of all, in 1801 he signed an agreement with the Pope called the Concordat. In the Concordat, Napoleon agreed to allow Catholics to worship freely again. In return, the Pope allowed Napoleon to appoint all the bishops in France and agreed that all priests should take an oath of loyalty to Napoleon.

As a result of the Concordat, priests were able to come out of hiding and churches re-opened. The religious conflict ended as quickly as it had started. This was another triumph for Napoleon, for it gave him the support of millions of people who had spent the last ten years hating the revolution.

Reforms

By 1802, Napoleon had made peace with Europe and ended the religious conflict at home. A grateful Senate increased his powers, raised his pay and made him 'Consul-for-Life'. Voters were asked to show what they thought of this. $3\frac{1}{2}$ million voted in favour, only 8,000 against.

Now that he had power for the rest of his life, Napoleon started to reform the way France was run. In 1802 he began a reform of the country's schools. The main change was the creation of a new kind of secondary school, the *lycée*.

Living under strict military discipline, pupils at these high schools studied a curriculum drawn up by the government. On leaving, they took an examination called the *Baccalaureate* for entrance to university.

Perhaps his greatest achievement was a reform of the French law into seven books called codes. He began in 1804 with a Code of Civil Law called the *Code Napoléon*. Codes of criminal and commercial law were added over the next five years. These codes simplified the very complex laws that had existed for centuries. They also made into law some of the things that revolutionaries had demanded in 1789. Individual rights, freedom of belief, and equality before the law were all included in the codes.

Napoleon becomes Emperor

In 1804 Napoleon increased his power still further by making himself Emperor. Again, voters showed their support with a massive vote of approval. France thus became an empire after twelve years of being a republic.

13 *The re-establishment of worship after the Revolution.* **A painting by Adam Topffer in 1810 shows villagers talking to their priest and putting the village cross back up.**

Find three things that people are doing in this picture which they could not have done during the Terror.

As Emperor, Napoleon brought back some of the things that had been abolished during the Revolution. For example, he insisted on being crowned in a coronation ceremony like that of the old French kings. The picture above shows the moment of his crowning when he took the crown from the Pope and put it on his own head.

Next, Napoleon brought back noble titles for members of his family. For example, his brothers Joseph and Louis became Grand Elector and Grand Constable of the Empire. Later, in 1808, he created an Imperial Nobility

14 ***The Consecration of the Emperor Napoleon I and the coronation of the Empress Josephine in the Cathedral of Notre Dame de Paris, December 2, 1804.*** **This gigantic picture (6 × 9 m) was painted by Jacques-Louis David between 1805 and 1807. Standing in the foreground, from left to right, are Napoleon's brothers Joseph and Louis, his sisters Caroline, Pauline and Elisa, and his sisters-in-law Hortense and Julie. Napoleon's wife Josephine is kneeling before him. Behind her, carrying her regalia on cushions, are four Marshals of the Army. Seated in an arch at the back is Napoleon's mother. Pope Pius VII, surrounded by bishops and cardinals, is sitting behind Napoleon. To the right in the foreground are leading ministers of the government.**

consisting of princes, dukes, counts, barons and knights. Nobles had to be very rich if they wanted to pass their titles on to their children: a prince, for example, had to leave his son an income of 200,000 francs a year to keep the title in the family. Unlike nobles before 1789, however, Napoleon's nobles had no privileges.

By 1804, therefore, the French Republic had been been replaced by an Empire, the Catholic Church had been restored, and people could become nobles once again. The Revolution was over.

Review and Assessment

1
  a On a full page, make a time-line showing what Napoleon did in each of these years: 1796, 1797, 1798, 1799, 1801, 1802, 1804. (You should be able to find about 12 events in this chapter.)

  b Which of those events do you think helped him most in his rise to power as Emperor? Explain your answer.

  c Are there any events on your time-line in which luck played a part in helping him rise to power?

2
Study sources 1 and 7. What do these paintings tell you about how battles were fought at the time of Napoleon?

3
What do sources 3, 4, 5 and 6 tell you about what definitely happened when Napoleon entered the Council in 1799?

4
Study source 14. What makes this scene a valuable source of evidence about Napoleon?

5
Study sources 8–12, then answer these questions:

  a How does source 9 differ from source 11?

  b Judging by sources 8, 10 and 12, which portrait of Napoleon crossing the Alps is more accurate – source 9 or source 11?

6
Look at sources 1 and 7, then read these descriptions of the artists who painted them:

      Source 1 was painted in 1845 by Henri Félix Philippoteaux (1815–84), a painter of portraits and historical scenes, engraver and illustrator.

      Source 7 was painted in 1801 by Louis François Lejeune (1776–1848), a general in one of Napoleon's armies. An amateur artist, he sketched many of the battles in which he fought, including those of Aboukir, the Pyramids and Marengo, and later painted them on canvas.

      Judging by this information, is one source likely to be more valuable than the other as evidence of warfare in the time of Napoleon? Explain your answer.

7
Look at sources 1, 3, 6, 9 and 14.

  a In what ways might these paintings not give a true picture of Napoleon?

  b Despite not giving a true picture of Napoleon, how can these sources be used as evidence of his rise to power?

4 Napoleon and Europe

The peace which Napoleon made in 1802 did not last. Britain, Russia and Austria formed another Coalition in 1805 and restarted their war against France. Napoleon's armies won that war and conquered half of Europe in the process. In the lands that they took, the French made great changes to the way they were organised and run. Many of the changes had long-lasting and important results. This chapter is about those changes.

Napoleon conquers Europe

Napoleon defeated the Coalition's armies in a series of battles in central Europe. In 1805 he smashed the Austrian armies at Ulm and Austerlitz (see map on page 70–71). When the Prussians joined the Coalition in 1806 he defeated them in the battles of Jena and Auerstadt. In 1807 he beat the Russians in the battles of Eylau and Friedland.

With three major enemies beaten, there was nothing to stop Napoleon enlarging his empire. In 1807 he made the Italian states of Tuscany and Parma into French provinces. In 1809 he took the Illyrian Provinces and the Papal States. And in 1810 he added Holland and north-east Germany to the empire. The map on page 70–71 shows all these conquests.

As well as enlarging the French empire, Napoleon made changes to the countries which shared a border with it. In 1808, for example, he occupied much of Spain. In central Europe, he forced the rulers of many small German states to join their lands together. This reduced the number of German states from 300 to thirty. Then, in 1806 he brought the leading German rulers together in a union called the Confederation of the Rhine, with himself as their

head. This union helped Napoleon by forming a barrier between France and its enemies – Austria and Prussia. The states in it also provided Napoleon with money and soldiers for his armies.

The rule of the Bonapartes

Napoleon could not personally govern all the land he had conquered. There was too much of it. He therefore shared it out among his family, for them to

1 *The Surrender at Ulm.* A painting of 1833 by Charles Thévenin shows the Austrian generals surrendering to Napoleon after their defeat in the Battle of Ulm in 1805. Behind them, columns of Austrian troops are being marched away into captivity.

govern. He made his brothers Kings of Holland, Westphalia and Spain. His step-son became Viceroy of Italy and his brother-in-law King of Naples. His sisters were given the smaller Italian states to rule.

The Bonaparte family made many changes to the states they ruled. They reformed laws that were out of date, got rid of feudal rights, took away land from the Church, and modernised the way their states were governed. In this way, French ideas about how to organise and run countries spread to many parts of Europe. The map on the next page shows these changes.

Napoleon's Europe: 1810

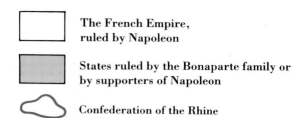

The French Empire, ruled by Napoleon

States ruled by the Bonaparte family or by supporters of Napoleon

Confederation of the Rhine

Kingdom of Holland

Ruled by Napoleon's brother
Louis Bonaparte from 1806 to 1810.
He:
• introduced a new, fairer code of
  criminal law
• helped farmers
• set up a Science Academy and a
  Royal Library.
(In 1810 Napoleon took personal control
of Holland after making it part of the
French Empire.)

Grand Duchy of Berg

Ruled by Napoleon's brother-in-law
Joachim Murat from 1806 to 1808, then
by Napoleon and his nephew Louis
from 1808 to 1814.
They:
• ended feudal rights and dues
• got rid of serfdom
• introduced the *Code Napoléon*
• reduced the power of the Church
• gave equal rights to Jews
• gave citizens equal rights.

Principality of Lucca

Ruled by Napoleon's sister
Elisa Bonaparte from 1805 to 1814.
She:
• modernised industry
• helped artists, writers and sculptors.

Kingdom of Spain

Ruled by Napoleon's brother
Joseph Bonaparte from 1808 to 1813.
He:
• ended feudalism
• abolished nobles' privileges
• closed many monasteries and abolished
  the Inquisition
• introduced a constitution allowing an
  elected parliament and giving people
  equal rights
• organised a new system of Law Courts
• divided Spain into regions
  run by Prefects.

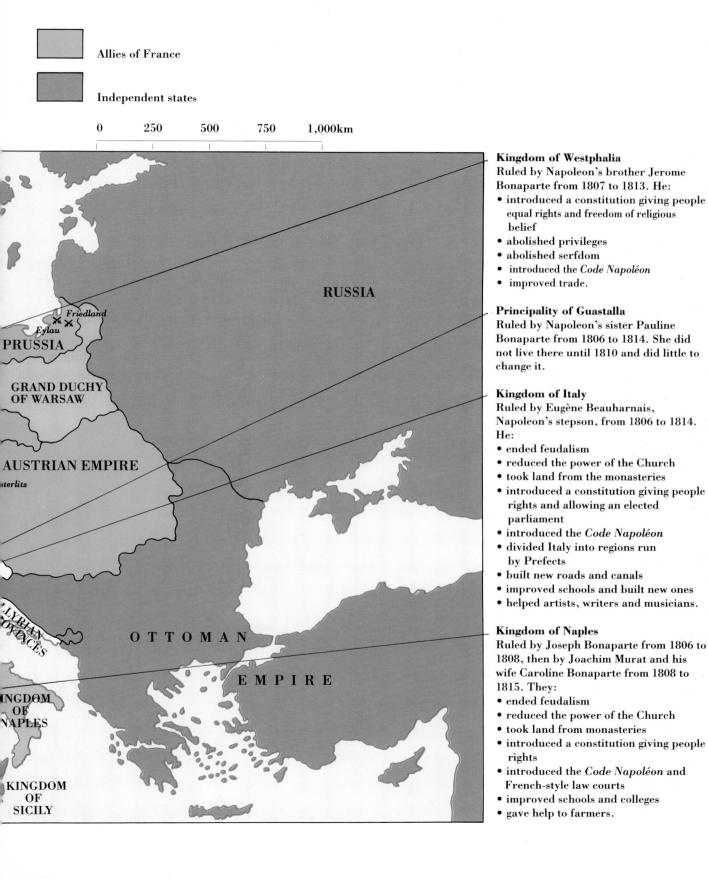

Allies of France

Independent states

| 0 | 250 | 500 | 750 | 1,000km |

RUSSIA

Friedland

PRUSSIA

Eylau

GRAND DUCHY
OF WARSAW

AUSTRIAN EMPIRE

sterlitz

ILLYRIAN
PROVINCES

O T T O M A N

E M P I R E

NGDOM
OF
NAPLES

KINGDOM
OF
SICILY

Kingdom of Westphalia
Ruled by Napoleon's brother Jerome
Bonaparte from 1807 to 1813. He:
- introduced a constitution giving people
  equal rights and freedom of religious
  belief
- abolished privileges
- abolished serfdom
- introduced the *Code Napoléon*
- improved trade.

Principality of Guastalla
Ruled by Napoleon's sister Pauline
Bonaparte from 1806 to 1814. She did
not live there until 1810 and did little to
change it.

Kingdom of Italy
Ruled by Eugène Beauharnais,
Napoleon's stepson, from 1806 to 1814.
He:
- ended feudalism
- reduced the power of the Church
- took land from the monasteries
- introduced a constitution giving people
  rights and allowing an elected
  parliament
- introduced the *Code Napoléon*
- divided Italy into regions run
  by Prefects
- built new roads and canals
- improved schools and built new ones
- helped artists, writers and musicians.

Kingdom of Naples
Ruled by Joseph Bonaparte from 1806 to
1808, then by Joachim Murat and his
wife Caroline Bonaparte from 1808 to
1815. They:
- ended feudalism
- reduced the power of the Church
- took land from monasteries
- introduced a constitution giving people
  rights
- introduced the *Code Napoléon* and
  French-style law courts
- improved schools and colleges
- gave help to farmers.

The costs of French rule

You can tell from the map on pages 70–71 that the Bonapartes tried to improve the states they ruled. This did not mean, however, that life was better for everyone living under them. Rule by the Bonapartes brought losses as well as benefits.

The biggest losses were caused by Napoleon's wars. Every state under the Bonapartes' rule had to provide troops for Napoleon's armies. The Grand Duchy of Berg, with a population of 50,000, had to provide 5,000 men in 1806. Westphalia, with a population of 2 million, provided 600,000 men, of whom 38,000 were killed or wounded. In all, half a million young Germans, Italians and Poles saw action in Napoleon's armies.

It wasn't only the young men of these states who suffered from the wars. The families they left behind also paid a heavy price. Fighting wars is very expensive, and Napoleon paid for his wars by taxing people. Roughly half his spending on war from 1804 to 1814 was paid for by foreigners living under the Bonapartes' rule. The German states alone contributed 560 million francs.

The French armies usually did not carry food with them on campaigns. They took the food they needed from the villages and farms they passed. Peasant families living near the route of a marching army had to put up with soldiers digging up their crops, killing their animals, and eating and sleeping in their homes. The picture below gives an idea of what it was like to have French soldiers living off your land.

3 **Soldiers of the French Light Infantry prepare a meal in their bivouac, or camp. A sketch by the artist Benjamin Zix who spent eight years in the French army.**

Resistance and rebellion

Many European people hated the rule of the French. Hatred was strongest in Spain, ruled by Joseph Bonaparte. In 1808, Spaniards rebelled against the French and began a war of independence against them.

The French went to great lengths to crush the Spanish rebels. A captain of the British navy, fighting on the side of the rebels, described how French soldiers dealt with one rebellious area:

4 The French . . . troops returned to Santiago . . . burning every village on their way back, and laying waste the country in every possible manner. There were no fewer than five priests of different parishes, and several hundreds of peasants, both male and female, put to death . . . Most, if not all, of the bodies . . . were either stabbed or deeply cut across the fingers or wrists; indicating apparently, that . . . they had been sabred or bayoneted by the invaders. Their wretched hands, being naturally held up to defend their heads, were the first to receive the blows aimed at more vital places.

Captain Basil Hall, *Fragments of Voyages and Travels*, 1832

The Spanish painter Francisco Goya, who travelled around Spain during the war of independence, also witnessed many scenes like that. He drew what he saw and put his drawings together into a collection called *The Disasters of War*. The picture below is the twenty-sixth drawing in the collection.

> **What do sources 4 and 5 suggest about French rule in Spain?**

5 Men, women and children, hiding in a cave, are shot by French soldiers. A drawing by Francisco Goya entitled *No se puede mirar* (One cannot look), from his collection *The Disasters of the War.*

Judging by the picture below, what difficulties would the Army of England have faced in its invasion of Britain?

The opposition to Napoleon

Napoleon and Britain

You can see from the map on pages 70–71 that five countries managed to stay independent of Napoleon. The most powerful and dangerous of these was Britain. Defeating Britain soon became one of Napoleon's highest priorities. Between 1803 and 1805 he gathered a massive 'Army of England' in camps along the Channel coast, ready to invade Britain. 2,443 boats were built to ferry 193,000 men and 9,149 horses across the Channel. But because it would take six tides to get them all out of port, the French needed control of the Channel for at least four days. Without that control, the invasion fleet could be attacked by the British navy while it was at sea.

Napoleon's admirals tried to lure the British away from the Channel by tricking their ships into chasing them into distant waters. Admiral Villeneuve, for example, led British warships under Admiral Nelson on a wild goose chase to the West Indies.

These tricks succeeded, but Napoleon decided in August 1805 to postpone the invasion of Britain. News reached him that an Austrian army was marching towards France. To deal with this threat, Napoleon ordered the Army of England to leave the Channel coast to cut off the Austrians in central Europe. The result was the Battle of Ulm on 20 October (see page 67–69).

Although Napoleon won a great victory at Ulm, he had thrown away all

6 Napoleon visits the port of Boulogne in July 1804 to watch the Army of England practising for its cross-Channel invasion of Britain. Although a gale was blowing that day, Napoleon insisted that the exercises must go ahead. 2,000 men were drowned when their boats capsized in the winds. A painting by J.F. Hué

hope of invading Britain. While the Austrians were surrendering to him at Ulm, Nelson's fleet trapped Admiral Villeneuve's fleet off the coast of Spain. In the Battle of Trafalgar on 21 October 1805, only nine out of thirty-three French ships escaped unharmed. This meant that the French navy now had no chance of controlling the Channel, thus making an invasion impossible.

The Continental System

With invasion out of the question, Napoleon tried a different kind of warfare against Britain. In 1806 he issued an order called the Berlin Decree, forbidding the states under his control to trade with Britain. His aim was to force Britain to surrender by ruining its trade. This blockade of British goods, known as the Continental System, led to an immediate fall in the quantity of goods imported into and exported out of Britain.

Although most of Europe belonged to Napoleon's Continental System, one country refused to join it: Portugal. Because much of Britain's trade was with Portugal, Napoleon decided to force it to join. French forces invaded Portugal in 1807 and occupied the capital, Lisbon.

The invasion of Portugal, however, soon led to unexpected problems for Napoleon. The Spanish, as well as the Portuguese, hated the French armies who marched across their land to seize Lisbon. They rebelled against the French in 1808 (see page 73) and began a war of independence against them.

Britain quickly joined in the fighting. British forces were sent to the Spanish peninsula to help the rebels fight the French. For the next five years, they fought the French in the 'Peninsular War'. For Napoleon, this war became a 'Spanish ulcer', using up huge amounts of money and keeping a quarter of a million of his soldiers tied down in Spain.

The Continental System created similar problems for Napoleon on the other side of Europe. In 1810 the Tsar of Russia decided to leave the System because it was damaging Russia's trade. He opened his ports to British ships and allowed Russian merchants to trade normally with Britain. Napoleon decided to force the Tsar back into the Continental System by invading Russia.

The Russian Campaign

Napoleon gathered a 'Grand Army' of 655,000 men and invaded Russia in the summer of 1812. The Russian armies retreated before this massive onslaught. After defeating them in the Battle of Borodino, Napoleon entered the capital, Moscow, in September 1812.

This looked at first like another great triumph for Napoleon. It was not. Only two months later his men were on the retreat. By the time they crossed the border back into Europe, only 50,000 were still alive. The Grand Army had been wiped out.

What had gone wrong? The sources which follow, taken from the memories of survivors, show some of the reasons for this disaster. Problems began as soon as the Grand Army entered Russia. As one soldier wrote in a letter, the Russians did all they could to stop the French from finding food:

> **7** Most houses stand empty and roofless . . . The houses have been ruined or ransacked, the inhabitants have fled . . . The streets are strewn with dead horses that give off a horrible smell now that the hot weather has come.
>
> Albrecht Adam, *From the Life of a War Artist*, 1886

This led to immediate transport problems for the French army. Napoleon's Master of Horses wrote in his diary:

> **8** The emperor was always anxious to obtain everything at the least possible expense and the result was that . . . everything had been loaded on waggons in the hope of being able to commandeer [take possession of] horses from the countryside. This had always been done in previous campaigns but in Russia there was no means of doing so. Horses, cattle, inhabitants had all fled and we found ourselves in the middle of a desert.
>
> Armand de Caulaincourt, *Souvenirs*, [Recollections], 1837

The lack of horses meant that the French had to dump huge amounts of their stores by the roadside. Food and medicine ran short. The situation did not improve even when they reached Moscow. The Tsar, his government and many of the people of Moscow abandoned the city, set it on fire as they went, and retreated to safety in the countryside. Napoleon did not have the time or the men to follow them. Nor could he stay in Moscow because he could not feed his army during the coming winter. He therefore ordered the army to retreat.

Winter, however, came early, and the French were unprepared for it. A British officer serving with Cossacks in the Russian army remembered:

> **9** Some Cossacks with me saw a gun and several carts at the bottom of a ravine, with the horses lying on the ground. They dismounted and, taking up the feet of several horses, yelled, ran, danced and made fantastic gestures like crazy men. Pointing to the horses' shoes, they said, 'God has made Napoleon forget that there was a winter in our country' . . . It was soon ascertained that all horses of the enemy's army were in the same improperly shod state . . . From that time the road was strewed with guns, carts, carriages, men and horses.
>
> General Sir Robert Wilson, *Narrative of Events during the Invasion of Russia by Napoleon Bonaparte*, 1860

10 *Marshal Ney during the retreat from Moscow*, a painting by Adolphe Yvon (1817–93).

As the French retreated, the weather got colder. In December the thermometer dropped twenty degrees below zero, and men froze:

11 I had gone all day with nothing to eat, and I spent that night – the coldest of any – without food, in a hut open to the wind, surrounded by corpses and huddled near a dying fire . . . This room was next to a huge barn and during that bitterly cold night between four and five hundred took refuge inside. At least three quarters of them froze to death, even though they had lain one on top of the other around several fires.

General Comte de Segur, *Mémoires*, 1873

As the winter set in, food ran out. According to a Russian general, starving, freezing men did desperate things to get food and warmth:

12 I saw a dead man, his teeth deep in the back leg of a horse which was still quivering. I saw a dead man inside a horse which he had disembowelled and emptied in order to crawl inside and get warm. I saw another man tearing with his teeth at the entrails of a dead horse. I did not see the wretched French eating each other, but I did see dead bodies from whose thighs strips of flesh had been cut away for eating.

General Count de Langeron, *Mémoires*, 1902

During Napoleon's six-month Russian campaign, 370,000 French soldiers died in battle, of illness or of the cold. A further 200,000 were taken prisoner; half of them died in captivity. 200,000 horses also died.

1 Using sources 7 to 12 as evidence, give as many reasons as you can why the French Grand Army was defeated in Russia.
2 Sources 7–9 and 11–12 were written by soldiers who fought in the Russian campaign. Does this mean they are all reliable sources of evidence? Explain your answer.
3 Picture 10 was painted by someone who was not there. Judging by sources 7–12, do you think it a realistic picture of the retreat from Russia?

The fall of Napoleon

Napoleon's defeat in Russia led to further disasters, for the Tsar of Russia now organised a new coalition against him. Russia, Sweden, Prussia and Britain joined together as allies in 1813 and soon drove the French out of central Europe. When they saw that the French were on the run, the Austrians and the German states joined the coalition. By 1814 the allies had driven the French right back into France.

With nearly every country in Europe against him, Napoleon was forced to surrender in April 1814. Allied troops marched into Paris and occupied it. Napoleon gave up his throne and the Allies set up a new government with Louis XVI's brother at its head. He was crowned as Louis the Eighteenth (XVIII).

Elba

The Allies allowed Napoleon to keep his title of Emperor but sent him into exile on the island of Elba, off the coast of Italy. For nearly a year, Napoleon ran the island as a little country. He created a tiny army and navy, opened some mines, and helped farmers to improve their land. But he soon became restless and unhappy. When he heard, after nearly a year there, that Louis XVIII was becoming unpopular, he decided to return to France. In March 1815 he secretly sailed from Elba and landed in southern France. Louis fled while crowds cheered Napoleon all the way to Paris, where he set up his empire again.

13 *In the valley of the shadow of death*: a cartoon of 1814 by the British artist James Gillray shows Napoleon being attacked by the British lion, the Russian bear, the Austrian eagle and the figure of death.

14 A different view of Napoleon in 1814: a painting from 1864 by the French artist Ernest Meissonier. Entitled *The French Campaign, 1814*, it shows Napoleon leading his army in a final defence against the advancing Allies.

Which of pictures 13 and 14 do you think best portrays Napoleon's situation in 1814? Explain your answer.

The 'Hundred Days'

Napoleon's second empire lasted just ninety-five days. The leaders of Austria, Britain, Russia and Prussia put together six armies of almost a million men and set out to crush him. Rather than wait for them to attack, Napoleon marched with 122,000 men to meet them in Belgium. He beat one of the Prussian armies on 16 June and then attacked the British army at Waterloo, in Belgium, on 18 June. The British, reinforced by Prussians, defeated his attack. Napoleon fled from the battlefield and returned to Paris.

Napoleon would have continued the war, but the Assembly wanted peace. Without the support of the leading politicians, Napoleon abdicated (gave up his throne) on 22 June. Two weeks later he gave himself up to the captain of a British warship off the French coast, just in time to escape the pursuing Prussians, who wanted to execute him.

Napoleon hoped that the British government would give him protection and allow him to live in Britain. It did not. He was not even allowed to get off the ship when it dropped anchor in Plymouth. He was transferred to another ship and taken to a place from which he could never escape, the island of St Helena in the South Atlantic, 8,000 km away from France. There, although he had never received a trial, he spent the rest of his life in captivity. He died in 1821.

Review and Assessment

1 When Napoleon was told that he would not be allowed into Britain but would be exiled to St Helena, he wrote a protest letter to the British government. This is part of it:

15 Bonaparte's protest

I hereby solemnly protest against this injustice . . . I came freely on board the Bellerophon. I am not a prisoner. I am the guest of England . . . I gave myself up in good faith and claimed the protection of the English laws. If this act is carried out [exile to St Helena], it will be impossible for the English to talk about their integrity [good name], their laws and their liberty. British good faith will have been lost . . . I appeal to history . . .

Napoleon
On board the *Bellerophon*
4th of August, 1815

16 Napoleon on the warship *Bellerophon*, watched by British naval officers. A painting by the Scottish artist William Orchardson.

a Judging by what you have read in Chapters 3 and 4, what do you think there was in Napoleon's history that made the British send him without trial into exile on St Helena, rather than let him live in Britain?

b Is there anything in Napoleon's history that makes you think he deserved fairer treatment than he got from the British?

2 Compare the map on page 54 with the map on page 70. Which countries changed as a result of the Napoleonic wars, 1800–1810? Which did not change?

3 On a full page, make a table like this. Use the information in this chapter to fill the boxes with short notes showing how some of the states of Europe changed as a result of Napoleon's wars.

	Changes in the shape of the states	Changes in the states' ruler	Changes in the way the states were run	Changes in the states' law, society, religion etc.	Changes in the states' relations with France
German states					
Holland					
Italian states					
Spain					

4 Do you think any of the changes you have shown on your table could be described as improvements? Explain your answer.

5 The legacy of the revolutionary era

The era of the French Revolution and Napoleon ended in 1815 but it did not stop being important. For many years to come, people all over Europe continued to feel its effects. In all sorts of ways, it helped to shape their lives, their beliefs and the societies in which they lived. This chapter is about that legacy of revolution.

Traces of the revolutionary era

If, in London, you walk through Trafalgar Square, visit Madame Tussaud's, or take a train from Waterloo Station, you are in the company of names that became famous as a result of the Napoleonic wars. Visit any French town, and you will almost certainly walk along streets named after famous generals and battles of the revolutionary era.

Those are only the most obvious traces of the revolutionary era that remain today. There are many others. Measure a metre, weigh a kilogram or pour out a litre, and you are using weights and measures invented by the revolutionaries in 1795. Look at the flags of the countries of Europe, and you will see that half are modelled on the tricolour flag of the revolutionaries of 1789 (see page 84).

But perhaps the most important traces of the era are the ones that cannot easily be seen. These are the ideas about how to organise societies that the revolutionaries passed on to future generations. Two sets of ideas were especially important. The first is known as liberalism.

DÉCLARATION DES DROITS DE L'HOMME ET DU CITOYEN. Décrétés par l'Assemblée Nationale dans les séances des 20, 21 23, 24 et 26 août 1789, acceptés par le Roi.

AUX REPRESENTANS DU PEUPLE FRANCOIS

1 The 'Declaration of the Rights of
Man and the Citizen'. The main
points are:

1 The 'Declaration of the Rights of
Man and the Citizen'. The main
points are:

1 Men are born and remain free
and equal in rights . . .

2 These rights are liberty,
property, security and
resistance to oppression . . .

3 The power to rule comes from
the whole nation . . .

4 Liberty is being able to do
whatever does not harm others.

5 The law only has the right to
prohibit actions harmful to
society.

6 The law should be the same for
everyone . . .

7 A man can only be accused,
arrested or imprisoned in cases
decided by the law . . .

8 The law must only require
punishments that are strictly
necessary.

9 Every man is innocent until he
has been declared guilty.

10 No man ought to be uneasy
about his opinions, even his
religious beliefs.

11 Every citizen can talk, write
and publish freely.

12 The public force [i.e. the police]
is for everyone's advantage, not
for the benefit of the people who
are entrusted with it.

14 All citizens have the right . . . to
have explained to them why
taxes are necessary, so that they
can consent freely to them, can
check how they are used, and
can decide the shares to be paid.

16 A society which does not
guarantee people's rights is a
society without a constitution.

17 Because property is a sacred
right, nobody can be deprived of
it, except in the public interest.

Liberalism

The French Revolution began, as you have read, when the Estates General of 1789 declared that it was a 'National Assembly' and set to work to write a constitution, which is a set of rules for how a country should be run. It began by making a 'Declaration of the Rights of Man and the Citizen', giving French citizens equal rights and liberties. Source 1 (above) shows what these were.

The idea of giving people liberty and equality through a constitution was one of the important achievements of the revolution. And when Napoleon conquered Europe in the 1800s, constitutions were introduced into the states

2 The tricolour flag.

that came under French control. The ideas of liberty and equality therefore spread throughout Europe.

In 1815, however, after they had defeated Napoleon, the old rulers of Europe took back their thrones. Many got rid of his constitutions and went back to ruling their states in the old way. But they could not wipe out people's memories of what it was like to be ruled with a constitution. Millions of Europeans became 'liberals', believing in the ideas of liberty and equality, and wanting a constitution giving them rights.

Nationalism

Another key idea of the French Revolution was that France was a nation, not a kingdom. In other words, France was not the personal property of King Louis XVI: it was a union of all 28 million French-speaking people. The first act of the revolutionaries was to set up a National Assembly to speak for these people. Soon after, they adopted the tricolour flag to represent the nation – the red and blue colours of the people of Paris combined with the king's traditional white.

During the Revolutionary wars, the French set up new nations in the lands they had conquered. Italian speaking people were brought together into nations such as the Roman Republic. Later, Poles gained their own nation when Napoleon created the Grand Duchy of Warsaw. Millions of Germans became citizens of new nations when Napoleon forced 300 German rulers to unite into just thirty states. Many European people thus found out what it was like to live in their own nation, and to be ruled according to a constitution.

This came to an end in 1815. Politicians from the countries that defeated Napoleon met in Vienna, capital of Austria, to redraw the map of Europe. At the Congress of Vienna, as this meeting was called, they re-created many of the old states that Napoleon had destroyed. Old royal families took back their thrones in Spain and the Italian states. A German Confederation of thirty-nine states replaced Napoleon's Rhine Confederation. Belgium, Holland and Luxemburg became a single Kingdom of the Netherlands. The new borders of all these states are shown on the map on page 85.

You can easily see from the map that the new borders of Europe had nothing to do with people's nationality. Millions of Italians were under Austrian rule, Poles under Russian rule, and so on. Napoleon and the French, however, had set an example that these people would not forget. Throughout the nineteenth century, people living under foreign rule, or living in separate states from their fellow countrymen, did what the French had done in 1789: they started revolutions to change the way they were ruled.

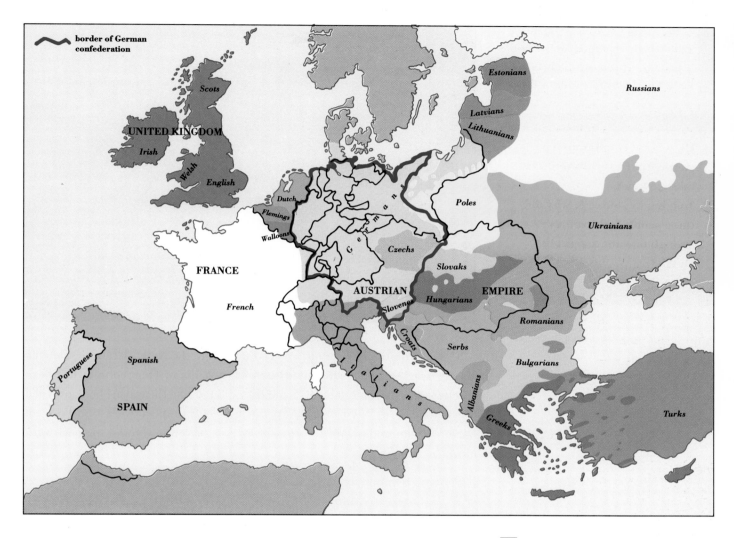

border of German confederation

3 Map of Europe in 1815.

2 Nationalists wanted people of the same nationality to live in one nation, or state.
What changes would have to be made to the map above if a) Italian, and b) German nationalists gained what they wanted after 1815?

Revolution

Liberals and nationalists started revolutions in 1820, 1830, and 1848. Sources 4 to 8 help us to understand what they were trying to achieve.

In the German states, many of the revolutionaries were students. One of them, Heinrich von Gagern, aged nineteen, wrote about their aims in a letter to his father:

4
Jena, June 17, 1818

. . . we want Germany to be considered one land and the German people one people . . . We want a constitution for the people that fits in with the spirit of the times . . . Above all, we want the princes to understand that they exist for the country and not the country for them.

Heinrich von Gagern, *Letters and Speeches*, 1815–48

5 Belgian revolutionaries march out of the city of Liège on 4 September 1830 to fight the Dutch in Brussels. A painting of 1880 by the Belgian artist Charles Soubre (1821–93).

1 How can you tell from this picture that a revolution was taking place?

2 Judging by source 6, why did these people feel strongly enough to want to fight the Dutch?

In 1830, revolutions broke out in six countries. In the Netherlands, the Belgian people rose in revolt against the Dutch King William. Their country had been taken over by the Dutch in 1815 and they did not like the way he had governed them since then. Their complaints can be seen in this conversation between King William and one of the revolutionaries who was allowed to speak with him:

6 'Sire, Belgium demands a free press.'
'But press freedom already exists' [said the King].
'Yes, Sire, in Holland but not in Belgium . . . There are other complaints that we have been told to bring to your Majesty's attention. All the big government offices are in Holland . . . The High Court of Justice is in Holland . . . Jobs in the civil service and the armed forces are reserved for the Dutch who see them as their birthright . . .'

Alexandre Gendebien, *Mémoires*, date unknown

King William, however, refused to listen to such complaints. Dislike of his rule spread throughout the provinces and people armed themselves to fight the Dutch. After much bloodshed, the Belgians drove the Dutch out and proclaimed that Belgium was an independent country.

A French magazine later summed up the aims of the 1830 revolutions in the cartoon on page 87. Europe is shown as a volcano which last erupted in 1789, destroying the castle in the foreground. Liberty is now erupting again from the volcano. Kings and their courtiers flee while new nations are formed by the lava of liberty pouring down its sides.

7 A cartoon published in the French journal *La Caricature* in 1833.

The countries of Europe were shaken by revolutions again in 1848. In the Austrian Empire, for example, Hungarian people rebelled against the Austrian authorities in Budapest. One young Hungarian drew up this petition, listing their demands:

8

What does the Hungarian nation want?

1 We want a free press and an end to censorship.
2 Responsible government in Budapest.
3 Annual meetings of the parliament in Pest.
4 Equality before the law in civil and religious matters.
5 A national guard.
6 Equality of taxation.
7 An end to feudal dues.
8 A jury system ...

Equality, Liberty, Fraternity!

Laszlo Dene, *The Radical Left in the Hungarian Revolution of 1848*, 1976

3 Judging by sources 4–8, what were the main aims of revolutionaries between 1815 and 1848?

4 Which of those aims can be described as a) liberal, and b) nationalist?

5 Which of those aims are similar to those of the French revolutionaries (see source 1)?

Images of revolution

The revolutionaries of the nineteenth century borrowed images as well as ideas from the French Revolution. The most famous of those images was that of 'Liberty'.

The image of Liberty was created in 1792. The revolutionaries who overthrew the king took it as the symbol of the new Republic. As picture 9 shows, Liberty was portrayed as a young woman. She is holding a club with which she has killed the many-headed monster of 'despotism'. In her other hand she holds a 'liberty cap'. Originally worn by freed Roman slaves as a

9 *Liberty*. **An engraving of 1792 by Jean-François Janinet.**

symbol of their freedom, the liberty cap became fashionable among *sans culottes* in 1792.

Marianne, as the figure of Liberty was named, appeared in countless pictures, statues and models throughout the French Revolution. She appeared again during the revolutions of 1830. The painting below, by Eugène Delacroix, shows Marianne leading revolutionaries over a barricade in a Paris street. She is holding the tricolour flag in one hand and a musket in the other.

Perhaps the most famous image of Liberty is the Statue of Liberty at the entrance to New York harbour (source 12). This 200 tonne, 97m high copper statue was a gift to the United States from the French people to show the friendship between their two republics. It was suggested by a French historian to commemorate the 100th anniversary of American independence.

10 *Liberty leading the People* by Eugène Delacroix (1830).

11 **The front page of an Italian socialist newspaper on 1 May 1901.**

12 *The Unveiling of the Statue of Liberty*, by Francis G. Mayer.

Marianne went on making appearances long after the revolutions of the nineteenth century were over. Picture 11, from the Italian socialist newspaper *Avanti!*, shows her leading workers in their struggle against their 'capitalist' bosses. And picture 13 shows a statue of Liberty made by student revolutionaries in China in 1989.

13 A statue of Liberty in Tiananmen Square, Beijing, in China in 1989. It was made from blocks of polystyrene by students at Beijing University who were demanding greater freedom.

How do pictures 9–13 show that the French Revolution continued to influence people long after it had finished?

14 A painting by Jean-Baptiste
Isabey, one of Napoleon's favourite
painters, shows Napoleon's coffin
being lifted onto the French
warship *Belle-Poule* in 1840 to be
taken back to France.

**1 Suggest what the artist wanted
us to think or feel when we
look at this painting.**

Legends and myths of revolution

The era of revolution created many myths and legends. The most lasting of
them was the Napoleonic legend.

Before his death in exile on the lonely island of St Helena, Napoleon
dictated his memoirs and encouraged his friends to write down everything he
said. In these writings he built up an account of his life and ideas which made
him seem like a great hero and a martyr. When these were published after his
death, they helped to create a reputation for him as a great historical figure.

In 1840, nearly twenty years after his death, the British government
allowed his body to be taken from its grave on St Helena for re-burial in France.
When Napoleon's coffin arrived in Paris, 100,000 people lined the streets in
freezing weather to pay their respects. He was buried in the Invalides church,
and was later transferred to a massive tomb made of precious stone. Since then,
more people have visited his tomb than any other tourist attraction in Paris.

What made Napoleon such a legendary figure? Why have so many people
heard about him and want to visit his tomb? Part of the answer can be found by
looking at the pictures of him that were drawn or painted at the time.

We can also find answers by looking at the monuments which were built
to honour his memory. The picture on page 93 show one of the most famous
monuments to Napoleon.

The legend of Napoleon spread in many ways. The Bank of France issued
20 franc coins bearing his portrait. Brands of cigars and fine brandy were
named after him. Even babies got to hear of him at their mothers' knee, as
source 16 shows. It is an English lullaby, written down in 1950 by a woman who
knew it from her grandmother:

**2 Look at the pictures of
Napoleon on pages 58, 60, 64,
68 and 74. What impression of
him do they create?**

15 The Arc de Triomphe in Paris. Built between 1806 and 1836, it is the largest triumphal arch in the world (50m high, 45m wide). It is decorated with carvings showing Napoleon's greatest victories. Over the shields at the top are the names of 172 victories that the French armies won during the revolutionary and Napoleonic era.

3 Which aspects of Napoleon's achievements does source 15 commemorate?

4 What similarities are there between this monument and the pictures of Napoleon you have studied in this book?

16
Baby, baby, naughty baby,
Hush, you squalling thing, I say.
Peace this moment, peace, or maybe
Bonaparte will pass this way.

Baby, baby, he's a giant,
Tall and black as Rouen steeple,
And he breakfasts, dines, rely on't,
Every day on naughty people.

Baby, baby, if he hears you,
As he gallops past the house,
Limb from limb at once he'll tear you,
Just as pussy tears a mouse.

And he'll beat you, beat you, beat you,
And he'll beat you all to pap,
And he'll eat you, eat you, eat you,
Every morsel snap, snap, snap.

Iona and Peter Opie, *Oxford Dictionary of Nursery Rhymes*, 1951

5 What image of Napoleon is created by the lullaby (source 16)?

6 How does it differ from the other images of Napoleon in this book?

7 Judging by what you have read in this book, are either of these images accurate? Explain your answer.

Review and Assessment

17 *Vive la Charte* (Long live the Charter). Revolution breaks out again in Paris in 1830 as liberals protest against the king's decision to suspend the French Charter or constitution.

1 Compare the picture opposite with picture 32 on page 20.
  a How many years were there between these two events?
  b In what ways were the two events (i) similar, (ii) different?

2 The people in picture 17 opposite were risking their lives to demonstrate in support of their constitution (the Charter). If you could have talked to some of them, what might they have said to explain this?

3 What connections were there between the changes that Napoleon made in Europe (see Chapter 4) and the revolutions that took place in Europe between 1815 and 1848?

4 With the help of sources 4, 6, 7 and 8 in this chapter, explain why many people in Europe took part in revolutions during the nineteenth century.

5 How do the following help to explain why millions of people joined in revolutions between 1789 and 1848?
  a The conditions in which they lived.
  b The ways in which they were governed.
  c The taxes they had to pay.
  d Their feelings about their country.

Index